*Ottakar's* LOCAL HISTORY *Series*

# Wilmslow

*The Victoria public house, Wilmslow. Once home to the local police force, the stone tablet with the words 'Cheshire Constabulary' inscribed into it can be seen above the door to the left.*

*Ottakar's* LOCAL HISTORY *Series*

# Wilmslow

*Compiled by
Heidi Reid*

OTTAKAR'S

TEMPUS

*Ottakar's bookshop, Wilmslow.*

First published 2002

Tempus Publishing Limited
The Mill, Brimscombe Port,
Stroud, Gloucestershire, GL5 2QG

British Library Cataloguing in Publication Data.
A catalogue record for this book is available from the British Library.

ISBN 0 7524 2678 8

Typesetting and origination by Tempus Publishing Limited
Printed in Great Britain by Midway Colour Print, Wiltshire

# Contents

# Foreword

Life is full of strange experiences. One of mine, which was totally unexpected, was to represent the people of Wilmslow in Parliament for four years. I found them to be kind, caring and not at all like the caricature of them as wine-guzzling, Ferrari-driving hedonists that occasionally appears in the wilder columns of the national press. It is true that the place has rather more wine bars than it needs, forming a cordon vineux round St Teresa, a Roman Catholic church, but their customers tend to be Wilmslow's visitors rather than its residents. It was one of my extra-parliamentary duties, as MP, to correct the caricature.

This book will do a much better job than I could. It belongs to a series of local histories published by Ottakars in places where it does business (and what a relief it is, in a town that has lost so many small shops, to have a good book shop at last!). Wilmslow isn't really a town, of course, but a constellation of villages and linked communities, each with its own diverse history. Some of that history is set down here by the best of historians – local people who know it because they have lived it.

I would hazard a guess that Wilmslow has seen more change in the past twenty years than anywhere else in Cheshire – certainly more change than most of its people would like. There's no way of reversing that process; but I would like to think that the spirit of Wilmslow persists through all the changes. You will find that spirit distilled and expressed in this book of living memories.

Martin Bell
September 2002

# Introduction

I am an interloper. Having lived in the North West for some fourteen years, I finally settled in 'the region' (Bollington to be exact), a mere five years ago, and prior to this book Wilmslow was a place where I worked and had spent the odd evening out with friends. Imagine then, the joys in store for me, as the weeks following my acceptance of the role of 'Editor of the Wilmslow Local History Book' began to unfold.

I was surprised to learn that Wilmslow had always been known, and in many quarters still is known, as a village – and not as a small town, as I had always assumed it to have been. I was even further surprised by the passion people feel for this place and the sorrow at which they received such recent developments as the pedestrianisation of Grove Street and the loss of the independent shops that survived there for so many years.

Through this book Wilmslow has come alive for me, it was a place of such community spirit, and, although perhaps less evident today than in days gone by, through it's many organizations, societies, churches and charities, still is. It was a joy to read accounts of the Wilmslow Carnival, the Rose Queen Parades, of Fulshaw Park and Lindow Common and of the rustic nature of 'old' Wilmslow. I learnt that Samuel Finney was more than just the name of a pub, that The Victoria used to be the police station, that Safeways supermarket is where the market square used to be and that Charnley's the Chemists is a survivor amongst a sea of modern chain stores.

I would like to take this opportunity to thank all the people who have spoken to me about Wilmslow, who have furnished me with a greater understanding of the place and who have provided me with the material needed to put Wilmslow on the page.

We asked the local community to 'Write Your Own Local History', and they have certainly done that – I hope that the material within these pages will remind people of the wonder of Wilmslow, teach those who don't already know the value of certain elements, and simply be a joy for everyone to read.

Heidi Reid
September 2002

*The Manager of Wilmslow Gasworks, William Severs, and family, 1902. Taken outside the Gasworks. Courtesy Mrs Gabrielle Acton.*

# 1 Wilmslow Remembered

## Living Wilmslow

*Prize-winner*

It's the noise that has changed. The peaceful, countryside sounds of my youth in Wilmslow have gone, replaced by the constant din of traffic both in the air and on the roads. I hear it all the time in Hawthorn Street, where I live. Many of the cars go past with radios blaring, so that I can hear them from inside my house, the louder the better seems to be the rule.

I am ninety-one years of age now, Wilmslow born and bred. My parents, grand-parents, and great grand-parents were also born in the village, we oldies never call it a 'town'.

How peaceful it used to be when I was a boy. From our house in Nursery Lane we could hear the clock at Fulshaw Hall chiming the hours away. Quiet then was something to be revered. People even put a load of straw on the road in front of houses where a sick person lay.

There were no macadam roads: stones or sets were the vogue. And there were very few cars. True, there were lots of crowing cocks, I can't remember when I last heard one. Almost every cottage had its own poultry, some even had a pig. We could also hear the screeching of the peacocks that were kept at Fulshaw Hall. But these were rustic sounds, and we rustics had to put up with them!

In my youth hares crossed the Alderley Road into Harefield, red squirrels scampered around in Fulshaw Park, sand martins nested in the banks of the stream that meanders through Alderley Edge golf course, and swarms of rooks commuted daily between Alderley Park and a tip at Cheadle - what a sight they made on windy days!

I once heard a corncrake up Jubilee Walk. The jubilee in question was that of Queen Victoria, after which the pathway was named. It doesn't exist now, but you can still trace its outline, along the front of the gardens on the grass-verged section of Bourne Street. Bourne Street, in those days, ran only from the Altrincham Road to Simpson Street. Jubilee Walk was made across the fields from the Simpson Street end of Bourne Street to Chapel Lane, opposite Nursery Lane, so that children who lived in Park Road could get directly to Fulshaw School.

That was the school that I attended. It was quite near the house in Nursery Lane where I was born in July 1911, and where I lived with my parents and my two brothers and one sister. Fulshaw then was more green fields than houses. Later, builders like Browns, Boones, Gibsons and others altered the face of Fulshaw completely. But when I was a boy there were numerous small farms in the district. Grove Farm, from where I used to deliver milk, was an exception. It was quite a big farm, standing on Knutsford Road, and the farmhouse is still there. Later, I used to drive cows from my grandfather's wheelbarrow farm in Hawthorn Street, up Beech Lane and Simpson Street, to the fields that he rented in and around what are now Bourne Street, Westward Road and Northward Road.

A wheelbarrow farm, by the way, was one that had no horse-power or machinery – a contractor was hired to carry out ploughing, harrowing, carting and other jobs that needed horses.

My grandfather's farm was situated where The Hawthorns old folk's home now stands. The only thing left now is the gnarled old holly tree that abuts the footpath on Hawthorn Street. Various histories of Wilmslow have carried a picture of this cottage – you can see the holly tree on it – and also one of my great-grandfather's thatched home – the Blue Bell pub-cum-farm – as it was then on Manchester Road half-way to Handforth.

*Len and Bea Willocks in the 1930s.*

*The Cottage, 87 Hawthorn Street, Wilmslow – where 'The Hawthorns' retirement home now stands.*

From the cottage smallholding on Hawthorn Street my mum told us that she used to deliver milk down Kennerleys Lane, which was then called Dirty Lane because it was so muddy.

My dad was educated at Chancel Lane School, which until recent years stood on the site of the public hall and car park near The Carrs entrance at the bottom of The Cliff road. He left when he was twelve. He could read, write, and recite the twelve-times table, and he could add and subtract – he said they couldn't teach him any more than that!

My mother went to the schoolroom on Chapel Lane, then the Congregational Chapel, now the United Reformed Church. Her father paid one penny a week for the privilege.

My paternal grandfather was born in a cottage, long since demolished, on Colshaw Farm, probably the biggest in the district, and now the Colshaw Estate. That cottage was portrayed by a local house painter who also had artistic leanings, and the picture now hangs in my daughter's home, which is also in Wilmslow.

My father started work at Colshaw Farm around 1887. He graduated from there to being a van man for Warburtons, then one of the biggest grocers in Wilmslow. They used to cover a wide area with their horse-drawn delivery vans. Dad eventually became a horse-man at Wilmslow Council, which, of course, used horses for many jobs.

Later, in the 1930s, he was made foreman over a number of unemployed men who were set to work to transform The Carrs into the public park you see today. It was the time of the Great Depression, and hundreds of thousands of men were out of work. I remember seeing the footpath in Nursery Lane, from Chapel Lane to the Post Office – a distance of several hundred yards – thick with men queuing for their dole money. Tradesmen – joiners, plumbers, brick-layers, painters, plasterers as well as office workers and others, were all victims at this time. Wealthy people of Wilmslow subscribed to a fund to provide employment for the workless, and the biggest project they were set to work on was to build footpaths through The Carrs Woods and into the parkland, and drainage across the fields to the River Bollin. Joiners came in handy to make a number of seats there. I can't remember the exact number of men thus employed, but I think it was between fourteen and twenty. I know that they worked for a fortnight, and then they stood down to give someone else a chance.

Dad was in charge of their work, and he was always proud of what was done there. Years later, after he retired, he was deeply upset when he learned that St Olaf's, the lovely little chapel in the woods, had been

*Colshaw Farm Cottages, Colshaw Farm, Wilmslow. (Courtesy Len Willocks)*

vandalised during and after the Second World War. Some people put the damage down to some of the thousands of RAF recruits who travelled to Wilmslow for basic training at the square-bashing camp on what is now the Summerfields housing area.

Back in my boyhood there was very little travel, apart from excursions into the surrounding areas on our bikes. Choir trips once a year meant a day at Blackpool or Southport. We used to look forward with great enthusiasm to any days out. The Foresters Friendly Society took us to Belle Vue, where we marvelled at the animals in the zoo, and then viewed the great firework displays in the evening.

We had a Stores concert once a year, too. The Stores was our name for the Macclesfield Co-operative Society. They had a big shop in Church Street. The concerts were held in the Drill Hall, then Wilmslow's chief place of entertainment. Dances, concerts, plays and even boxing matches were held there. The Drill Hall was behind where Safeways store now stands, on what was then the market square.

It was there that the weekly market was held, much bigger than the present-day one. During Wakes Week the market square was given over to a funfair, with dobby-horses, swing boats, a shooting gallery, coconut shies, and, one memorable year, a motor-cycle wall of death – quite a sensation at that time.

Then there was the Wilmslow Carnival, at one time reputed to be the biggest one-day carnival in England, with a mile-long parade consisting of horse-drawn tradesmen's vehicles, brass bands, jazz bands, clowns, dancing troupes, comedians and fancy dress. Oh, it was a great affair.

The first carnival that I remember took place in Holly Road North, in a field, loaned, I believe, by Mr Paulden, of Paulden's store, Manchester. He then lived at Green Hall, since burnt down. Later the carnival committee bought the field on Altrincham Road that is still called the Carnival Field.

The Alderley Edge and Wilmslow Flower Show before the Second World War was a very big event, and nurserymen from all over England and even from Scotland exhibited there. This too was supposed to be the biggest one-day flower show in England. It was renewed after the War, but was never as big as in the 1920s and '30s. Then, in addition to the show itself, every year a first-class brass band played there – Fodens, Black Dyke Mills, Besses o' the Barn, and others. It really was a great event. I was a gardener for most of my working life, and was proud to serve on the committee from 1930 and for several years after the war.

We also had the old wooden Picture Palace, situated on Swan Street, where we saw all the old silent films. We saw Tom Mix and Buck Jones in Westerns, Charlie Chaplin, Harold Lloyd and Buster Keaton in comedies, as well as Pearl White in The Perils of Pauline, and the Fu Manchu serials.

The by-pass that now takes traffic past the Rectory towards Alderley Edge did not exist then. In those days, the main road from Manchester came up the hill and turned sharply right, down Swan Street and through Grove Street. In earlier times, before my day, traffic had to pass a toll house where Barclay's Bank now stands.

I often wonder what Wilmslow was like, long before even my great-grandfather's time. I don't know of any place of its size that has so many Greens within its boundaries. I make it six in all: Morley, Davenport, Alcock, Parsonage, Lacey and Finney. Alcock Green no longer exists, but up to the nineteenth century it used to be in the area of the present-day Ashcroft, between Knutsford Road and the Stockton Road end of Fulshaw Park.

Wilmslow is not mentioned in the Doomsday Book, and that is not surprising, as Wilmslow Parish Church was not built until after AD 1200, and it is general knowledge that the church gave its name to the village. Prior to that time, I believe it is probable that the greens would have existed as individual hamlets.

These five greens would, no doubt, have had cottages close by and our forefathers probably grazed their cows, goats, donkeys, perhaps, and poultry there. For many it would have been subsistence living.

*Len Willocks at ninety years of age, with his great-grandchildren, June 2002.*

Some families would have found work at the various large houses in the district. Fulshaw Hall was built around 1200, and the long-vanished Bollin Hall dated from around 1250 – it is said that Anne Boleyn stayed there. It was demolished around the time when the railway viaduct was built in the 1840s.

The original Hawthorn Hall was also medieval. The present fine building, on Hall Road, dates from 1698. In later years my father claimed that a young man called Gladstone was educated there, perhaps laying the foundations for when he later became Prime Minister. There were also Norcliffe, Pownall and Green Hall.

The people may have lived around in their separate hamlets, but they would have had to get to the parish church each Sunday. Anyone who failed to do so could find themselves in severe trouble, perhaps the least of their problems being that on their death they could not even be buried within the confines of the parish. That is what happened to the conscientious objectors like Quakers. You can still find their seventeenth-century graves near Graveyard Farm on the outskirts of Mobberley. So it is not surprising that most of the hamlets, or greens, gradually became merged with what we now know as the centre of Wilmslow, as over the years more and more people set up home nearer to the parish church.

Changes are always taking place, and some, especially in recent years, do not seem to me to have been for the better. But the old Wilmslow Urban District Council motto – roughly translated from the Latin – was 'our fortunate dwelling place', and I still believe that Wilmslow is a pleasant place in which to live. But if only I could hear again the sounds of my youth!

*Len Willocks*

# Jottings by Jessie, a lifelong resident of Bourne Street (1907 – 1995)

*The following childhood memories were jotted down by Jessie Acton (née Worsley) about a year before her death in 1995. Her daughter, Mrs Jean Gould, very kindly submitted them, alongside photographs of Jessie and her family.*

*Jessie's mother Mollie.*

I was born on Sunday 25 August 1907, at number 11 Bourne Street, Wilmslow. My earliest recollection is of swinging on our front gate waiting for Miss Myrtle Sumner to pass on her way to and from the local school held at the Congregational Church Rooms in Chapel Lane. She always spared time to stop and speak to me, and I eagerly waited for the day that I could start school! When that day eventually arrived, a new school building had been completed in Wycliffe Avenue, and there, at the age of four, I could see my beloved Miss Myrtle five days a week.

My uncle and aunt and their family lived in the caretaker's house, which was handy for me. I remember my auntie being allowed to give drinks of milk to the children who walked each day from Mobberley and Styal and who brought sandwiches with them. The more local pupils went home and were allowed one and a half hours for lunch.

I remember Mrs Singleton, the head of the infants, and also Miss Edna Sumner. Best of all I recollect Mr Thomas, head of the senior school, who was very kind; particularly when I had to refuse the scholarship to a grammar school in Stockport at the age of eleven because my mother was a widow and could not afford to let me go. I was in Mr Thomas' class for four years.

*Jessie's Uncle Fred who sent a hare on the train from Whitney, Oxfordshire.*

*Jessie Worsley, aged about four years.*

*Jessie's mother and family – from left to right: Molly (Jessie's mother), Auntie Annie, Aunt Lizzie, Uncle George and Grandmother Pritchard.*

I was very pleased to receive, on two occasions, the sum of five shillings for a full year's attendance and punctuality from the 'Oak Charity'.

On Sundays I attended Fulshaw Church School in Nursery Lane, which was in the charge of Miss Smith, whom I found terrifying most of the time, although I changed my opinion somewhat when she escorted a few of us to Manchester one Christmas and treated us to tea and cakes at Lyons Corner Café and then to the theatre to see *A World of Happiness*.

As children we played outside a lot in Bourne Street and spent hours playing skipping and hopscotch and marbles and other games as there were no traffic problems in those days.

I had a cousin in the Cotswolds who owned a toyshop, and once a year she would send us a boxful of dolls' house furniture that kept us busy in the dark evenings as we repaired all the damaged pieces.

One day we received a telegram telling us to meet a certain train at Wilmslow Station where we discovered that my uncle had put a hare in the Guard's van. Mother, who was a wonderful cook, soon got busy, and our neighbours were delighted to help us eat it!

Saturday evenings were always eagerly awaited, as a neighbour who worked at Victoria Station in Manchester brought some herrings or mackerels from the market, for which my mother usually paid him two pence. On Thursday, a Mr Hulme came round the area with a churn of buttermilk and we would go out with a jug for a gill or pint. Milk was delivered twice a day, a jug with a note was put on the window sill and that would cost us two pence a pint. The rag and bone man came once a week and exchanged our rags for either a balloon or donkey stone (for cleaning the door step).

When I was seven, the district nurse came to live with us from Germany, apparently for work experience. She was very small and rode all over the district on a large bicycle. If I ever tried to leave anything on my plate at dinner she would say, very severely, 'Where I have been today, they would be very glad of that', making me feel very ashamed.

In the autumn a man, who rented a plot on the bog at Saltersley Common for half a crown a year, would come down the road with a cart loaded with neatly cut pieces of peat, and we would buy so many to store in the coal house for lighting fires in the winter.

We would sit around the fire at night making rugs with pieces of material we cut up as we went along, or knitting gloves and black stockings. One winter I recall knitting combinations and vests for children in the skin hospital in Manchester, for which I was rewarded with an invitation to their Christmas party.

I had less happy memories of Pendlebury Children's Hospital, when I accompanied my mother, who had to take my brother Horace to have treatment for his hip which was infected with tuberculosis. The only way this could be done was by scraping the bone, which was very painful for him; the sound of his screams down the hospital corridor upset me so much that I never forgot them, even long after he died.

I saw the seaside for the first time when I was six. Great-Aunt Emily, who was housekeeper to a wealthy cotton family in Manchester, took my cousin and me to Blackpool for a whole week. I remember paddling in the sea, wearing black and white rubber-backed bloomers, making sand pies, and having donkey rides. Other summers saw my mother taking us on the train to

*Church Street, Wilmslow, with Auntie Annie's (Antrobus) shop on the left-hand side.*

Shrewsbury. We must have travelled on Tuesdays because when we arrived we then walked to the market hall where Aunt Lizzie, mother's younger sister, was selling eggs, butter and flowers (Tuesday being market day). By the time auntie had sold out, Uncle George, Mother's unmarried brother, arrived in his trap, pulled by Bonnie the horse, and took us to the farm at Baschurch, a few miles north of Shrewsbury. Auntie always seemed annoyed that her brother had bought yet more sheep! We received a warm welcome from Grandma when we arrived, and she would give us a good meal. We loved helping to collect the eggs and feed the hens, ducks and pigs. Uncle would not let us go too near the cows and sheep. I remember Jim, the youngest farm worker, setting mole traps and showing us where to pick bilberries.

The return home at the end of the first visit, I remember, was marred by a long delay on the train as other trains loaded with soldiers from nearby Prees Heath Camp were given priority over us. It was not until then that we realised that war with Germany had started; there had been no wireless or newspapers at the farm. On our eventual arrival back at Wilmslow Station we hurried down Church Street to visit Mother's elder sister, Auntie Annie, who

19

was busy selling paraffin and household goods in her shop. Our five cousins were in the living room at the rear and were all busy discussing the war and which relatives would be conscripted. Ahead of us lay rationing and other worries – life would certainly change from now on.

*Jessie Acton*

## Carnivals, cows and caramels

My mother, born in 1895, lived as a child on Manchester Road, Wilmslow, between Mill Lane and Hill Top.

In the house next-door's garden lived, in a ramshackle hut, Stephen Beswick, known locally as 'Jarmug'. He was full of tales of his time in prison and his experiences on the treadmill - a form of punishment.

Around five o'clock in the morning the sound of clogs past the house meant the workers were on their way to Styal Mill.

At the age of fourteen my mother became a telephone operator, with around 100 subscribers in Wilmslow. The telephone exchange was in a tall, narrow, white house in Grove Street, which in later years became a small café next to Woolworth's, nearly opposite the top of Grove Avenue. When there was a General Election results used to be relayed to the telephone exchange and then shouted out of the window to the waiting villagers!

If a fire broke out when my mother was young, a buzzer was blown from the fire station, and all the volunteer firemen raced to the station whilst horses were seized from cabs or wagons to pull the fire engine to the site of the fire. Local plumber, Andrew Price, was the Fire Chief, and at one fire he was diligently smashing windows when a

voice shouted from the ground, 'Go to it Andrew, good for trade!'

Wilmslow Carnival was a big event with a fair on the Carnival Field and a parade that collected money for the Alderley Edge Cottage Hospital. The parade contained decorated horse-drawn floats, bazooka bands, local adults and children in fancy dress, groups of dancers and acrobats. The St Bartholomew's Brass Band took part, as did the famous Hazel Grove twins who never smiled and collected money in up-turned umbrellas. A one-legged man hopped all the way along the procession route, without support, with his collecting box.

In my own childhood between the wars, Wilmslow was very rural and where I lived, on Chapel Lane, I only knew one family who owned a car. Playing whip-and-top on the road in Chapel Lane was unhindered by traffic as was racing with orange boxes on wheels. Cows came along the unpaved footpath from the small farm to the field, which is now Lindfield Estate. Any gate left open saw the risk of a cow in the garden!

The butcher's shop in Chapel Lane had a slaughterhouse behind it, and the squealing pigs, followed by blood in the gutters, was all part of life.

Sunday school treats consisted of going to Redesmere on the local coal merchant's lorry, sitting on chairs that were roped on to the back! Sunday School walks took us down to St Bartholomew's Church with the girls carrying flowers. After a short service it was tea in the Parish Hall and races on the Rectory field. To close the proceedings Miss Burman, from an elevated position in the Rectory garden, threw caramels to the children waiting below.

*Mrs Dorothy Ward (Née Warburton)*

*Dorothy Ward's great-grandparents, George and Ann Eden (née Holt), the year of their Diamond Wedding Anniversary, 1929. They farmed at 'Big Brick Hill Farm', Hough Lane – now 'Paddock Hill'.*

*Grove Street, Wilmslow, looking towards Alderley Road. (Courtesy* Wilmslow Express*)*

*Grove Street, Wilmslow, looking towards Bank Square. (Courtesy* Wilmslow Express*)*

# 2 People

## Every picture tells a story

Tucked away in a corner in Wilmslow Parish Church, on the floor, is a fifteenth-century brass. Brasses are not common in Lancashire or Cheshire. This one is the oldest. It is much worn by feet, having been for centuries in the middle of the chancel, and has no doubt been subject to much polishing as well. In a good light however it can still be made out very well. It is a medieval betrothal or a marriage. The youthful couple are shown holding hands, and charmingly solemn they are too. The man has a Henry V haircut, like a pudding basin. His other hand is raised to his heart. He is girt with a long sword and dressed in full plate armour with all its joints and hinges portrayed, but with no helmet. His spurred feet rest upon a thin hound who looks up at him reproachfully. The woman is as tall as her husband, with elbow-length wavy hair and a slightly cross-eyed look. She wears a long flowing dress with a plunging neckline, with a loose cape or shawl tied at her breast. A little lapdog sits at her feet on the folds of her dress. He is Sir Robert del Bothe, or plain Robert Booth, and she is Dulcia, or Douce Venables; a sweet name. Although depicted in youth the inscription, or what is left of it, records their deaths; she in 1453, he in 1460, 'on whose souls may God have mercy. Amen.'

Of all the people who have died over the centuries and been buried at St Bartholemew's only four or five are still there in a visible sense, their bodies preserved, in image at any rate. So what was so special about them? Why was it felt necessary that Sir Robert and Lady Douce should still be there, still holding hands, so long after their deaths? The clue I think lies

*Illustration of the fifteenth-century brass in Wilmslow Parish church of Robert Booth and Douce Venables, dated 1460.*

in the fact that she died first, and in the historical knowledge that she was the important one. He, before their marriage, was nobody much, certainly not here in Wilmslow. To find out why she was important we have to backtrack.

In 1402 three children were playing in the Bollin, as children like to do given half a chance. We don't know where exactly, which is a pity, except that it was 'near Ringway'. Perhaps it was in the deep pool near Oversley Ford, a favourite spot until the second runway came along. The children were Richard, Alice and Douce. He was eight years old, Alice four and Douce only two. How it happened we don't know, but Richard, the eldest, was drowned. Their father, Sir William Venables, Lord of the Manor by his marriage to Joan, the last of the Fittons, had died earlier that year aged only twenty-six. So Richard, by medieval law, was heir to the title and Lordship of all the lands of Chorley, Hough, Morley and Wilmslow, Styal, Dean Row and Fallibroome.

Two tragedies in one year, what was to be done? What was to happen to the inheritance? In an unusual settlement it was divided equally between the two surviving sisters. Alice got Chorley, Hough, Morley and Wilmslow, Douce got Styal, Dean Row and Fallibroome – they have remained separated ever since. The sisters, being now notable heiresses, attracted suitors. In May 1409 there was a double marriage, presumably here in Wilmslow Church. Alice, who was only eleven, married Edmund Trafford, and Douce, aged seven, married Robert Booth. So the brass pictures of Douce and Robert are portraits neither of their old age nor of their marriage, although there is something childlike about them.

These medieval child weddings were not as inhumane as they might seem. True they were arranged by their parents and were financial and dynastic contracts, not love matches, but the partners could repudiate the deal when they grew up, and it was only in 1421 when Douce came of age that the marriage was confirmed and the division of Wilmslow made final.

Edmund Trafford and Robert Booth were both knighted in consequence of their marriages, and their two dynasties held the divided lands until very recently. The Booths of Dunham, later Earls of Stamford, held Douce's half into the 1850s. The de Traffords held and administered Alice's half until the 1930s at least. Both the Booths and the Traffords were absentee landlords, their homes at Dunham Massey and at Trafford Park. This is why there is no Great House at Wilmslow, for once the lands were divided the ancient Manor House of the Fittons, Bolyn Hall, was allowed to fall into decay. In due course both landlords encouraged development in the area, which is why Wilmslow and Alderley Edge look like they do.

Names last the longest. Stamford Lodge on Altrincham Road marks an outpost of Douce's share, the Booth and later Stamford half of Wilmslow. The Trafford Arms in Alderley Edge village is the southern limit of Alice's and Edmund Trafford's half.

So what was the brass for? To remember Robert and Douce certainly, but any memorial can do that. Surely Robert ordered it to be made and set up after Douce's death, but probably before his own, as a reminder for every one to see of his claim and that of his descendants, to half of the parish and manor of Wilmslow. Because it was in the right of his wife Douce, the wedding was the important thing. The brass picture of Robert Booth and Douce Venables was put there because it was needed. They were both needed, in bodily form, to testify to the right to the property and Lordship in perpetuity – they still had a job to do.

What about the Trafford half? On the other side of the main altar is a dumpy stone effigy of a medieval priest lying on a simple stone tomb. Although he belongs to a later generation he represents the other side of the bargain, for he is Edmund Trafford, Rector of Wilmslow. He built the chancel of Wilmslow church in 1522, which is why he lies half in it and half in his own Trafford chapel. He died in 1536 having been Rector for nineteen years. He lies as he would have stood at the altar in life, hands held together in prayer. He has a priestly haircut, the circular shaven crown called a tonsure. His head rests on a huge clasped tome which must be the Bible, or perhaps a missel, the Liber Usualis, is more likely. He is fully robed and ready to celebrate Mass,

with a long hooded alb reaching nearly to his feet, a frilled chasuble over his shoulders, and the essential thin scarf-like stole. Round the top of the tomb a black letter inscription can be made out, painted not carved, and on the edges of the pages of the book is the ghost of yet more writing – surely there are traces of gilding here too? This all leads to the suspicion that this man was once painted all over, face, hair, robes and feet, all lifelike. The effigy of Humphrey Newton in a nearby niche bears this out, for he has definite traces of colour, red for his robe and black for his sleeves – so we can begin to get a picture of how splendid Henry Trafford would have looked, and how unavoidably present his body, life sized and life coloured, with his name and position in life written round his tomb for those who could read and represented in the glowing heraldry of the Great East window, for those who could not, must have seemed.

*Illustration of the stone effigy of Henry Trafford, Wilmslow Parish church, dated 1537.*

Why was it so important that he should remain so vividly present after his death? With hindsight we know that the Mass was not to be celebrated here in the same way for much longer, for England was on the brink of the reformation and soon the Puritans would come breaking glass windows and smashing effigies, although not his one – perhaps with his paint stripped off he became anonymous. But not knowing the future, the intention was surely that Henry Trafford would be present at every Mass that was celebrated in his holy chancel, present in body almost as a living celebrant.

It may seem fanciful to regard these ancient pictures and sculptures as anything more than commemorative works of art. But who has not felt the urge to communicate with a statue or a portrait, by touching them perhaps, or, when nobody is listening, by talking to them? Who knows how many lonely vergers and church cleaners over the centuries have got into conversation with Robert or Douce as they did their polishing? How many priests and people as they stand at the altar rail have cast a sideways glance of sympathy at Henry Trafford? And who knows what they all get up to when the church is locked up for the night?

*Matthew Hyde*

# The Romany people of Lindow

'On a summer's day in 1908 a horse-drawn Gypsy caravan wanders along the open road at a gentle pace. Toad watches entranced as the old bow-topped van is forced into the ditch by a horn-blasting motor car. "O bliss," he mutters. "O poop-poop".'

This scene from Kenneth Grahame's classic tale of the English countryside, *The Wind in the Willows*, records the beginning of Toad's obsession with speed and fast cars. It is also the beginning of the end for an ancient way of life.

In the film version of Graham Swift's novel *Last Orders* the recently widowed wife, played by Helen Mirren, is sitting on a bench reminiscing with an old family friend, played by Bob Hoskins. They are discussing happier times, when they all spent their holidays hop picking in Kent. 'Do you remember the Gypsies?' asks Hoskins. The question is followed by a misty flashback, showing a beautiful Gypsy girl, raven-haired and barefoot, feeding a plump brown baby on the steps of her vardo. Mirren's face lights up. 'Ah, the Gypsies!' she sighs. Researching the Romany presence around Lindow, I asked the same question of many elderly local residents and it always evoked that same response – a combination of affection and wistfulness for colourful characters with a way of life long gone.

The Gypsies came to Lindow Moss for centuries – some itinerant, but many settling permanently in the network of 'green lanes' which criss-cross the region. They became part of the local landscape.

Mainly of Welsh origin, the Gypsies gathered at Delamere had travelled to Lindow in convoy. They were 'black as berries, hair and skin', and lived in the traditional horse-drawn bow-topped vans. Upon arrival the first thing they did was to run chicken netting round the van and let the hens out.

After dark they set their horses to graze in adjacent fields and took them out at first light. If you got up early enough you could catch them! They galloped their horses round the Common and some lived on Lindow Common – where the monument now stands. They stayed there permanently, not just passing through. One Newgate resident remembers her mother's tales. 'One Gypsy had a bear called Venus and he went to Congleton with it at fair time, about 1895, not long before they were turned off. That Councillor got himself on the plaque when they re-opened the Common. That's good, it was never closed.'

An ex-Eton schoolmaster, Bower Alcock, built and lived at Bowers Folly, Greaves Road. His friend was a barrister, Herwald Morris. In the 1950s in an attempt to rid Morley Green of gypsies they pulled a bluff by erecting a notice saying 'No Movable Dwellings Allowed Here. Anyone Disobeying this Notice will be Fined'. There was, in fact, no existing law under which anyone could be prosecuted.

Gypsies lived in all the green lanes around Morley and Wilmslow. Strawberry Lane, Gore Lane, Hard Hill at the top of Moor Lane – they were all full of Romany caravans, some permanent, some transient. At the top of Racecourse Road is Greaves Road, which is still a green lane. This was a traditional stopping place for the Gypsies. On the corner by Sandy Lane are two small enclosures, apparently unloved and unused. The hedges are ancient and old fruit trees still blossom in spring. I suspect that this was Cabbage Mary's who 'looked like a Gypsy and grew fruit and vegetables which she sold at the gate'.

Facing the Common, they built the Workhouse on Altrincham Road in 1773, partly funded by money left to the parish for charities, which was lent on mortgage at $4\frac{1}{2}$%. After its closure it was run as a tenanted farm, shared by tow families. During the 1920's Gypsy Amos Smith and his family lived as tenants at Workhouse Farm, alongside George and Bertha Brown. Bertha was also a

*Lindow Common, Wilmslow.*

27

*Gypsy Amos and family at Workhouse Farm, c. 1920. (Courtesy Stella Willett)*

Brown (unrelated) before her marriage and her father, Levi Brown, started Brown's the Builders at the Rookery, near the station. Stella Willett, their granddaughter, was the last person to be born at Workhouse Farm. She still recalls the stories her grandmother told her. From the 1860's-1880's Granny Bertha used to visit the old Gypsy Queen on the Common. Held in great reverence, she sat on the steps of her van smoking a clay pipe, dispensing free advice and selling herbal cures and ointments.

Cyril Woods, of Newgate, clearly remembers Amos, who married his great aunt. He obviously made a lasting impression on the young boy:

'Old Amos was a big, handsome fellow. He dealt in horses. When he died my mother said she'd never seen so many Rolls Royces as there were at his funeral. They came from everywhere. Young Amos, his son, worked for Masseys in Alderley Edge. He married Marion Woods and they had two daughters. The Gypsy men always stood stock still, arms folded across their chest, just watching. When all the locals were skating on Black Lake, one gypsy fellow used to stand watching. Only his eyes moved. They loved brass and copper. Inside the vans there was brass everywhere. Horse brasses and suchlike.'

Standing still and silent in the green lanes it is easy to imagine their presence. One can almost hear the distant voices and the horses; smell the wood and peat smoke of their night fires. Gypsy children gathering medicinal herbs from the hedgerows for Her Highness's cures. The mothers selling fortunes and pegs and potions door to door, whilst the men got on with their horse-trading activities.

Gypsies also lived on what is now a small tree plantation at the very top of Moor Lane, beyond Ned Yates Garden Centre. There was another encampment near Horticon. Behind the Boddington Arms site the men cut willow and birch withies to make clothes pegs. The women visited two or three local tips. One was down Kings Road and is now the site of the Rugby Club. Another was down Strawberry Lane. From these tips the women collected empty sardine tins, which they cleaned before cutting the metal into thin bands with which to bind the two wooden strips together. When the Gypsy women called round hawking their pegs they were treated kindly by local residents, some giving them 'a crust for the baby' or cast-off children's clothing, and paying 4d per dozen for the pegs.

In the late nineteenth century the daughter of the family then living at Saltersley Hall was courting a Gypsy boy. When her parents refused to let her marry him he put a curse on the family, firing a rifle shot into the front door of the Hall and declaring that 'none of their heirs would thrive'.

Saltersley is so named because the men bringing salt from the Cheshire brine pits used to stop there overnight. They exchanged their exhausted pack horses for fresh ones with the gypsies, who took the salters' horses and restored them to soundness. Saltersley was principally a horse-trading post and nothing to do with salt smuggling, as legend has it.

In 1879 the astonishing Paleolithic wall paintings were discovered in the Altamira Cave in Santander province. By 1884, just five years after the discovery of these

*Bridle path used by the gypsies, leading to Pownall Hall and the tip from which the gypsies collected sardine tins – now Kings Road. (Courtesy Stella Willett)*

*Lindow Common and the surrounding racecourse, c. 1880. (Courtesy Ordnance Survey)*

Euskarian cave paintings we find William Norbury delivering a lecture to the Lancashire and Cheshire Archeological Society. His chosen subject was 'Lindow Common as a Peat Bog – Its Age and Its People'. In his lecture he posits the claim that the original inhabitants of Lindow – the Ancient Britons – were Euskarian Stone Agers and that those who now lived around these marginal, unwanted lands were their descendents. He refers to their 'dark Moorish skin, high cheek bones and leaden aspect. They were sly and suspicious and aggressive and "lungeous". The fiercer kind would bite like bulldogs. They shunned society and appeared destitute of religious instincts. Buck stealers, poachers and fishers. Basket works and beehives. Pugnacious squatters.' These unsubstantiated claims were made when moves were afoot to drive out the Gypsies. Was he deliberately confusing them? Did he really mean the Romanys?

Designated a national Site of Special Scientific Interest (SSSI) in 1963 and a Local Nature Reserve (LNR) in 1987, Lindow Common is the pride and joy of Macclesfield Borough Council, supported by the Countryside Commission and English Nature, but it is Racecourse Road, which surrounds Lindow Common in an almost complete circle, which brings us to historically more interesting territory. It may also hold the clue as to why Alderman John Royle saw fit to buy the Common and donate it to the residents of Wilmslow.

Exactly eight furlongs – one mile – in length, the racecourse was a dirt track circuit used for horse racing. It had been created by the Gypsies, to enable them to put their horses through their paces and show off their mettle. Their horse trading was conducted around Lindow Common, drawing people in from the surrounding areas.

According to Earwalker: 'In front of the workhouse is the Racecourse, where races are held during the Wakes, the last week in August. These races, which are of a very inferior character, do much harm to the neighbourhood and are in a fair way of being permanently discontinued'. Definitely not Royal Ascot! This was Lindow's version of Appleby Fair and, as far as the local burgesses were concerned, the horse races attracted unruly and undesirable elements. By 1896 the Gypsies' racing days were numbered.

'Many years ago a Local Committee unsuccessfully endeavoured to get absolute

*Hawthorn James Price and the darling of Appleby Fair – The Collier, best Romany stallion in the country!*

control of Lindow Racecourse, after which the Wilmslow Urban District Council took the matter in hand, supported by a monster petition from the ratepayer's association, containing 1,500 signatures. The petition was duly forwarded to the legal advisers of the lords of the Manor, accompanied by a letter from the Council asking for an interview on the question, which request was granted. The Council appointed a Deputation – we met on the fifth day of October 1896 – the Council finally suggested terms which were accepted. Hence the question which had so long agitated the public mind was forever settled. At a Special meeting of the Council on the fifth day of March 1897, a letter was read out by Mr E.H. Prior, Assistant Clerk, from John Royle Esq, of Northwood, Wilmslow, containing an offer to pay the purchase money for the land, and present the same to the inhabitants of Wilmslow to be used as a Recreation Ground forever. The Common has been enclosed by private subscription, and can now be protected from all encroachments.'

*Andrew Pearson*
*Wilmslow Past & Present*, 1897

Phew! Just in the nick of time for Queen Victoria's Diamond Jubilee on 22 June 1897, celebrated in Wilmslow with huge processions, brass bands, fireworks and the gifting of Lindow Common – historically common land – to the good people of Wilmslow! The monument commemorating this great event was erected in the centre of the very spot where the Gypsies had always camped. It is still there.

The outbreak of war in September 1939 brings us to Lindow Farm. The introduction of rationing quickly put paid to travellers and itinerants. To obtain a ration book one needed a permanent address. Many vagabonds and tinkers were taken to the Arclid Workhouse. Others, squatting in huts and shelters around the margins of Lindow Moss, were re-housed by the local authorities. Since Lindow historically belonged to the Gypsies, or vice versa, thirty-nine families were rounded up by the Manchester authorities and sent back. A Romany family usually consists of three generations, so this was quite a lot of people.

The fields in question sloped steeply down – the land was part of a sand hill and useless for grazing. Prior to the outbreak of war Stretford Motor Cycle Club used it for scrambling, but in October 1939 there was a knock at the farm door. Three Gypsy men handed farmer George Spragg a note from the Inspector of Police in Manchester. The fields were to be requisitioned. The note said 'Mr Spragg, you are to take thirty-nine families and you will receive 2/- per week ground rent for each family.' The Romany's had returned.

George Spragg's daughter, Mabel, grew up at the Lindow Farm and has clear memories of the gypsies who lived alongside them for the duration of the Second World War. Water was fetched from the well pump and cooking was done on fires in the open air with a 'chitty box' from which was suspended the old black cauldron pots containing boiling bacon – making huge ssoups. They had ration books like everyone else. The only nuisance caused was damage to some boundary hedges by the taking of wood for the fires. The horses were tethered on the lower slopes of the fields.

One of the families was that of Doris Shaw, a niece of the Collins family –

fairground people still extant. Tragically, her ten-year-old son died of meningitis and was given a Gypsy funeral. Their caravan, together with all its contents, was burnt. No longer classified as 'traveller', the bereaved family, presumably free to leave, walked away never to return.

Three generations lived in each bow-topped van. The old men slept under an awning erected alongside, also in sling hammocks strung underneath the vans. When the war ended they left in dribs and drabs, many to Wales, others went down south. Some went to the Middlewich area, where they remain. True Romany's, now owner occupiers on their own controlled site, which is scrupulously clean and well maintained with brick built toilet blocks and mains electricity to each van. They own six acres of land. Hawthorn James Price, aged seventeen, leads a typical Romany life and is passionate about their horses, of which they have 100. The Collier, a gorgeous seven-year-old cob stallion, is Hawthorn's pride and joy and amongst the Romany horse traders reckoned to be the best stud in the whole country. When I visited the site Hawthorn was preparing for Appleby Fair in June, his newly painted 'sulky' ready for the big race.

No longer free to roam, the Gypsies appear to have combined the best of the new without sacrificing their traditional way of life. In her eighties and failing, one Grandma has her own large Roma-van alongside that of her family, who look after her round the clock. Elderly Gypsies don't end up in nursing homes. 'No one else is going to look after my mum' said her son, explaining why they would be missing Appleby Fair this year.

*Christine Pemberton*

# Out in Wilmslow with Romany

When, in 1938, the Reverend George Bramwell Evens and his wife, Eunice, were seeking a home to live in following his recent retirement from the Methodist ministry, they passed, that December, a sign advertising houses for sale in the (then) village of Wilmslow. Proximity to the BBC studios in Manchester was a prime requirement at this time in his life, for his place as a firm favourite on the Northern Children's Hour on the wireless had led to the extension of his *Out with Romany* naturalist programmes to *All Regions*.

Gibson's the builders were developing an estate near the centre of Wilmslow and the individualistic style of the houses, plus the retention of many trees on the estate, caught the imagination of the couple. Having always lived in church-owned manses, the excitement of acquiring and furnishing their own first home was only slightly tempered by the talk of war. However, their moving-in during the first week of September 1939 coincided with the declaration of hostilities against Germany and, indeed, before the unpacking was finished; two small girl evacuees from Manchester arrived on the doorstep.

Not far away an RAF camp was under construction, destined to house 5,000 young men, and over the next few years Romany and Eunice welcomed more than 150 members of the forces as visitors to their home.

Romany was in demand for his personal lectures to audiences all over the country, so was often away, but the value of those talks, and his broadcasts in inspiring, and importantly, comforting listeners, was immeasurable. Eunice, in the authorised biography of her husband: *Through the Years with Romany* (University of London Press, 1946), quotes a letter from a bombed-out family in Gorton, Manchester, struggling to make a home in a strange district, describing how one afternoon, when morale was very low, the wireless was switched on and *Out with Romany* was announced. The writer describes feeling 'as though the sun had come out, that they were sharing a warm, happy feeling and that the world was not such a bad place if people like Romany were in it, and she cried like a child for the joy of finding a friend again.' Eunice, when sitting in the audience at his lectures, describes watching the harassed faces of the people around

*The Reverend George Bramwell Evens - 'Romany' - and his beloved companion Raq.*

her being 'transformed as he took them into a new world of wonder and beauty.' She recognised that he could be described as doing 'war-work of the highest importance.'

Romany and Eunice shared the duties of voluntary air-raid warden so that cover was available in his absences, and with his disinclination to attend meetings and lectures relating to their task, left Eunice to manage that side of the activities. He listened avidly to the daily wireless bulletins, which, at the start of the war, frequently contained bad and depressing news, and Eunice tells how, even as enemy planes flew overhead, hearing the call of an owl to its mate, or seeing the steady glow of stars, or the brightness of the moon, beyond these harbingers of evil, his spirits would be lifted.

Ready at all times to don his tin-hat at the first wail of the sirens, he was not always to be found in his appointed place. Eunice tells of the one and only incident of the war directly affecting their warden's sector. On Christmas Eve 1940, when the pilot of an enemy plane dropped his load within fifty yards of their house, Romany, seeing fire in the distance, rushed out, disregarding the possibility of unexploded bombs in his path, telling her to telephone the police, and June, their daughter, to prepare the first-aid equipment. As Eunice guided the local rescue party across the field one of them said 'the house is not on fire' and she immediately felt guilty as she had asked for the fire service to come. However, another rescuer pointed out that the blitzed house's bedroom fires could catch at any minute, so these were dealt with immediately, while Romany was helping the occupants to scramble out through a window as well as comforting the maid, who was trapped in her room, until the rescue party brought her to safety. Eunice felt that, rather ironically,

*Front cover of* Through the Years with Romany, *written by his wife Eunice Evens.*

their sector's wardens acquired a reputation for being exceptionally efficient and capable, whereas this isolated incident had been dealt with by their most un-businesslike warden long before even those on duty had arrived on the scene. Her only cause for concern at the time had been that, because the house's fires had been put out so quickly, the fire engine, when it arrived, had careered all around the village looking for the reported fire and found none in sight.

The homeless neighbours stayed with the family at Parkway for several months, and that Christmas Day was remembered as a most happy one, not least when Eunice saw 'Romany crossing the field carrying a turkey and other delicacies which he had unearthed from beneath the ruins.'

Romany had built an air-raid shelter at the side of their house in Parkway, which the family slept during raids and which he was to use as his 'den' thereafter. Ever resourceful, he also seized the opportunity to use debris from the demolished house as mortar rubble for his plants, and also to increase the fortifications of the shelter. His garden became his refuge from the stresses and strains due, not only to wartime itself, but also to the constant influx of visitors and evacuees. He described the opportunity to convert a 'rough, uncultivated wilderness' behind his house into a plot with the nearest he could get to a feature representational of Cumberland hills, a rocky outcrop, as having brought him most joy during his time in Wilmslow. Eunice tells of the amount of time and energy he put into this task that brought him so much happiness.

So, who was this man, Romany, who had chosen Wilmslow as the place to spend his retirement years?

Born in Hull in 1884, George Bramwell Evens's parents were running the Salvation Army mission there. His mother, Tilly (née Smith), was a traditional Romani, the sister of the evangelist and preacher, Gipsy Smith. He displayed an interest in the countryside from an early age, and this subsequently coloured his whole life. While based in Carlisle in 1921 he fulfilled a long-held dream to own a vardo (Romani for wagon). He and his loyal wife, Eunice, found one at the Brough Hill fair, which they purchased for £75. A hired horse named Comma, reputed to be so named as he never came to a full stop, drew it to their yard in Fisher Street, where they subsequently refurbished it and kitted it out for use as a mobile home.

*The Vardo - set in the Memorial Garden next to Wilmslow Library.*

One of the most vivid memories of Eunice at this time was when, after painting both the inside and the outside of the vardo, the roof's turn for attention came:

'So eager were we to finish that even a heat-wave would not stop us. The climax came when, clad only in our swimming suits, overalls and sand-shoes, we climbed up to felt and tar the roof. It was so hot that it was impossible to kneel down – but we had to finish it at all costs. The tar ran everywhere except where it was meant to go, and we spent half our time un-sticking ourselves and our shoes from the roof'.

The vardo was to play an enormous part in their lives, not only as their refuge for holidays, with son Glyn, daughter Romany June and Raq the Cocker Spaniel, but also as a feature in Romany's broadcasts on *Children's Hour* and in his writings as a gifted journalist and author of many outstanding popular books, one of which, *A Romany in the Country* has recently been re-published in large-print format by Isis and also as a talking book by Soundings Audio Books (read by the Romany Society's Patron, Terry Waite CBE). Many of the visitors who have made the pilgrimage to see the vardo in subsequent years have spoken of it having been 'a lifetime's ambition to actually be inside the vardo', a few shedding a tear as their childhood memories flood back.

Busy in the garden after breakfast on 20 November 1943, shovelling leaf-mould into his wheelbarrow, and chatting to a neighbour and two children, Romany complained of a pain similar to one he had experienced a few weeks previously, and went to rest. Half an hour later, Eunice discovered that 'this vitally alive man had been taken from this world'. At the age of fifty-nine his death shocked the nation. Eunice's scrapbook contains records of both BBC announcements and countless tributes in national and local newspapers. Everyone felt they had known Romany personally and to this day visitors recall their sadness at their loss. Unknown to most people, his appearance had belied a constitution which was not strong. A particular source of concern to his followers was that Raq the dog was pictured in one newspaper 'pining for his master', resulting in hundreds of enquiries about Raq's future.

Sadly, because the memorable broadcasts on *Children's Hour* of Romany's adventures in the country accompanied by the two 'little girls' Muriel and Doris (in reality two 'aunties' called Doris Gambell and Muriel Levy, accomplished broadcasters in their own right) were in those days done 'live', only one recording exists of an *Out with Romany* programme, the copyright of which rests with the BBC.

However, Romany's memory lived on, and in 1946, after the vardo had been brought to Wilmslow and placed opposite the house in Parkway, a 'Romany Society' was formed, at one time having 2,000 members in all parts of the country. These were only a few of the people who considered Romany so special: he had been a gifted communicator. His rich, deep voice, combined with a calm unhurried manner, made him able to gain the interest of, and impart his extensive knowledge of country matters and wildlife to all kinds of people, of all ages. On a platform he would hold attention by means of 'lightning sketches' (for he had a considerable gift for drawing and watercolour painting) and a well-developed sense of humour. All of these qualities ensured a compelling, never-to-be-forgotten, experience for the listener.

Thousands of names and addresses were recorded of people of all ages who had come to visit the vardo. At the suggestion of her neighbour, Mrs Anne Geake, Eunice presented it to the Wilmslow Urban District Council, with sadness, but with joy also, as the arrangements for it's opening to the public could be shared. Plans at this time were made for a special site to be created in Romany's memory where the vardo would be placed, and after prolonged post-war effort to raise sufficient funds, on 20 May 1950 the Romany Memorial Garden was opened by Councillor F. Parker, and the Memorial Stone was unveiled by Muriel Levy and Doris Gambell.

Pilgrimages continue to be made to the vardo but, perhaps inevitably as the organizing committee grew older (and a country-wide organization was difficult to maintain in the days before the technological benefits we now enjoy) the Society faded away after 1965, and local government reorganisation in 1974 saw the vardo placed under the care of the newly created Macclesfield District Council.

Following vital repair and refurbishment in 1992, restored to its original condition, the vardo took on a new lease of life under the direct management of the Council's Leisure Services department. Prior to its return to Wilmslow from the Macclesfield workshop, the vardo spent two days as part of the Council's stand at the Cheshire Show at Tatton Park, winning a special Cheshire County Council tourism award of a silver salver for the refurbishment work and prompting much interest, and the following day saw John Craven and a BBC team spending a day filming the delicate re-positioning in the Romany Memorial Garden, in readiness for transmission as part of the BBC's popular *Countryfile* programme.

Regular Saturday afternoon openings once a month during that summer brought steady streams of visitors and continued for four years until 1996, when the Romany Society was revived, with Mr Terry Waite CBE as Patron and Mrs Romany Watt (Romany June, Romany's daughter) as president.

One Wilmslow festival saw Keith Clifford (known to many as a Sony Radio Actor of the Year Award winner, for appearances in *Coronation Street*, and latterly as a key character on television's *Heartbeat*) give an enthralling one-man performance of a specially-written play by local television scriptwriter John Chambers called *The Saint and the Sinner* – Romany being the saint. Keith, who has an uncanny likeness to Romany, has also given a character performance at the vardo to Romany Society members at one of their general meetings.

With more than 300 members, the Society works with the Macclesfield Borough Council, as the guardian of the vardo and the holders of the Romany archive, to continue the summer openings and to arrange special events of interest to Society enthusiasts. A book service is operated for the sale and acquisition of second-hand Romany books (all out of print apart from the recent large-print publication mentioned previously) and once a year, in October, a weekend gathering is held, usually in Cumbria or Yorkshire, for members to 'walk in Romany's footsteps'. Badges and garments are available for purchase. However, the Society's prime aims include promoting the interest of young people in everything Romany held dear, offering awards to enable children's attendances at appropriate courses and events. On this theme, the Borough Council's Rangers complement the Society's activities on vardo open days, with displays and a series of 'Romany Tales' for children, and share the guiding of visitors to the garden.

In the same year that the Memorial Garden was opened, another memorial to Romany was erected at Old Parks Farm in Cumberland, where his ashes had been scattered six years before, consisting of a bird-bath made of Cumberland stone, standing on a little hillock amongst the wind-swept fells and woods.

After the death of Raq in 1947, a small memorial stone to this children's favourite was placed near the vardo, and is now next to that of his master in the garden in Wilmslow. To this day many people have a dog named Raq.

Eunice Evens died in 1978 and Glyn the following year, Eunice of course having been the right-hand woman throughout her married life, and Glyn having written two Romany books after his father's death.

But the Evens family talents live on - amongst them Romany June, who after service in the WRNS acted with the Royal Shakespeare Company at Stratford-Upon-Avon, then had triplets, and subsequently took up a career as a respected journalist, Romany Bain, now living in London, but still active as the Society's Presidents. One of the triplets, Roly, is an ordained Church of England minister and also a trained clown, bringing his own unique skills as a 'holy fool' to televisions and church congregations countrywide. Whilst Ben Watt, son of Romany June and her jazz musician husband Tom Watt, with his partner Tracy Thorn, form the singing duo 'Everything But the Girl', their song-writing, composing and performing skills having taken them to the top of the UK and US charts.

Many people have described the enormous impact Romany's philosophy has had

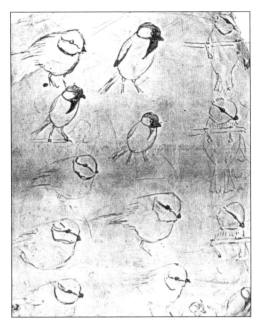

*Some of Romany's 'Lightning Sketches'.*

*Romany's memory lives on - a meeting of the Romany Society on the steps of the Vardo. Romany June is pictured centre with Olive Ambrose on the left.*

on their lives, passing downwards through the generations, so that grandchildren are now sharing, and sometimes learning to read with the aid of Romany books which their grandparents still treasure. Individuals have spoken of his legacy, including Sir David Attenborough, David Bellamy, Terry Waite, Eric Robson, Joan Bakewell and the *Daily Telegraph*'s Gillian Reynolds. A recent comprehensive and valuable review of Romany's works by Jonathan Briggs in the January 2002 edition of *Book and Magazine Collector* ponders the thought that he has been largely forgotten by the BBC. 'This seems curious,' he says, 'as the Corporation's subsequent success with natural history broadcasts would suggest a considerable debt to Evens.' But others feel that the success of the thriving Society might be the indicator that the appreciation of their hero is still strongly felt, feelings that were perhaps not fully expressed at the time of his death, due to other wartime interventions.

One aspect of Wilmslow's heritage remains, however: no one has yet challenged the belief that Romany's caravan is the smallest tourist attraction in the country.

*Olive Ambrose*
*Romany Society Committee Member and*
*Membership Secretary*

# Careers

'He wanted to go – and to arrive. Just the trudging up Twinnies Hill made him lag behind the woman. 'Come on! Stop yer dawdling!' Only temporarily reduced the gap. They emerged from the tree-canopied hill into the first real light of the day – Monday, 24 September 1917. Who would he be working with? Doing what? The woman knew he was entranced by the thought of working the new Northrop looms but only experienced men did that – not fourteen-year-old boys. 'You'll be all right', she said, 'They're all very friendly'. This was not his impression from listening to her conversations with his dad.'

Robert Burgess (1718-1854) was the pre-industrial cottager so admired by William Cobbett. Robert and countless relatives had long lived on the edge of Lindow Common, known as 'The Bog', where around his Foden Lane, Chorley home he kept a few animals and poultry, set potatoes, dug peat and cut thatch. His stand-by employment was very occasional brick-making (behind Folly Cottages on Knutsford Road) and, more frequently, the whole family activity of cotton handloom-weaving. He and Martha, (née Astle) (1786-1847) had eight children, their births extending in somewhat leisurely fashion over twenty-four years. As Robert was one of eleven children, a substantial Burgess colony had been established in the northern end of Great Warford, in Chorley Lindowside (then part of Wilmslow) and in Fulshaw Lindowside. Some, mainly younger members, were moving north to Morley Lindowside. Handloom weavers reaped some benefit from the mechanisation of spinning up to the 1830s but the gradual extension of the mill-based power loom, as well as technological and organizational changes in farming, spelled the end for the rural cottage-centred handloom weavers. However the relative steadiness of mill wages was only a theoretical attraction, whether at the nearby cotton, later crêpe, mill in Mobberley (by the Roebuck Inn) or at Greg's Mill (Quarry Bank, Styal). The Burgesses had enjoyed a proud, though often illusory independence. The mill would have been a dreadful fate. Anyway, better times could have been just around the corner. So the older men hung on. They told the census up to 1881 that they were handloom weavers, but the reality was different; they were labouring in the brickyards, on the roads or on the farms of the Hough. Three of Robert's four boys moved from one labouring job to another – short-term hiring, often by season. The remaining son, Robert Jnr (1821-1890) began work at home as a ten-year-old bobbin-winder for his mother and father; at twenty he was a handloom weaver. His family joined other Burgesses and their close friends and relatives, the Moores, in a move to Morley, where most became labourers. The mill at Styal, now much closer, had little attraction for them.

However, some of their children were breaking ranks in their quest for a more secure wage. One of these was Elizabeth Moores (1823-1905) of Morley Gorses (by today's Lindow Common) who worked through the 1840s as a reeler and winder at Greg's. She was the daughter of John Moores (1796-1869), a handloom weaver, who had left behind, in Chorley, his father John Snr (1775-1859). There had already been marriage links between the families; John Moores Snr was a cousin of Robert Burgess Snr. Elizabeth's job did not deter Robert Burgess Jnr; they married in 1847 and moved to a small terraced cottage on Eccups Lane, Morley. Robert persevered nominally with hand weaving but, with Elizabeth giving birth to Samuel in 1848 and returning to Greg's the following year, it would seem that Robert, with no in-house labour and probably no profitable demand for cloth, was seeking labouring jobs.

Many Wilmslow labourers worked at the Alderley Edge mines during a brief copper

*Andrew Burgess (1854-1917). Father of Bertha Burgess.*

*Amelia Burgess (1861-1925) (nee Cash Lewis). Mother of Bertha Burgess.*

*Joseph Acton (1880-1955), husband of Bertha (née Burgess), c. 1920.*

boom in the Crimean and American Civil Wars. With other branches of the family, Robert and Elizabeth moved to Pepper Street (Hawthorn Street) from where, after 1859, Robert walked to the workings of the Alderley Edge Copper and Lead Mining Company. Elizabeth continued to walk to Greg's; subject to short enforced breaks as four more boys were born, headed by Andrew Burgess (1854-1917). As labouring families moved from one rented property to another, branches of the family 'huddled' as neighbours, so that older children and older adults could child-mind during the long working days. Significantly and ironically, Robert, in his Census response of 1861, gave up his hand-weaving title and owned up to copper-mining, at the very time that

Elizabeth moved up to power looms, accompanied by young Samuel. Robert was far from attracted to mill life; thoughts of the bell, the deductions for lateness and other misdemeanours, the noise and the extra hours to make up for loss of production arising from drought or flood – all these reinforced his determination to stay out. He often told his family how he could not have faced constant supervision and the lack of opportunity to make up one's own mind. He was a conservative and a radical, standing out against what others dubbed progress, but which many like himself saw as little better than the workhouse. Greg's was something to fall back on only in desperate times. True, there were generations of loyal workers, many able to appreciate the Greg benevolence but the wages books show a considerable turnover of labour, with many working short spells around lengthy breaks that cannot simply be explained as maternity breaks for the increasingly female workforce.

Not surprisingly then, none of Elizabeth's boys enjoyed a mill career (Samuel was soon to become a railway man). When copper mining faded, Robert and Elizabeth continued to sample life in varying areas of Wilmslow, living next at Kennerley's Cottages (at the junction of Kennerley's Lane and Water Lane), then in Lacy Green and finally in the newly-built River Street, from where workers could walk to Greg's or, in their case, to a new and growing generator of jobs – the Handforth Printworks (along the River Dean to the east of the railway viaduct) which employed 152 workers in 1871. In 1890, Robert died in River Street, having seen out his time as a labourer, road mender and night watchman. He had been proud of his house, approached by steps and, with its cellar,

*Bertha Burgess (1883-1968), aged eighteen years.*

more roomy than the terraced houses farther along the street. The space, however, was needed; there was the widowed Elizabeth, son Andrew (1854-1917) and his wife and the first four of their six children. It was Andrew who worked for many years at the printworks, describing himself in the census precisely and rather grandly as a soap-boiler.

Andrew's wife's background was unusual, though in Victorian times, far from unique. She was Amelia Cash Lewis (1861-1925) whose mother was – almost inevitably – a Burgess - Sarah Burgess (1829-98). Sarah was a cousin of Andrew's who, in 1849, had married James Cash (1826-87), another handloom weaver-turned–labourer, and had set up home in Dungeon Fold at the back of the gasworks (between Church Street and Hawthorn Grove). They had a pre-marriage child who died in 1853, a son Charles who died at a few months old in 1852 and a second, Charles, who died at seventeen in 1871 – by which time Sarah had transferred her affections and James had departed to live next door with his mother Esther, a re-married widow, now Mrs Esther Percival. The new light in Sarah's life was her lodger – a genuine title while James was still there but a euphemism thereafter. Shoemaker William Lewis (1822-1884) from Weston, near Wem in Shropshire, was one of a growing army of 'Shroppies' seeking work in Wilmslow. The liaison with Sarah was serious and long-lasting, producing no fewer than nine children, brought to a round figure by the adoption of a Shropshire boy in 1877. They lived in Church Street, the newly-constructed Bollin Walk, the New Road (Manchester Road), Green Lane and Lacey Green where they were neighbours of Robert and Elizabeth Burgess before the latter moved to River Street.

Robert's second son, Andrew, thus married Amelia, 'the girl next door' – someone who continued to have a hard time battling against the prejudice shown towards the children of the liaison. Her mother, Sarah, called 'single woman' when presenting the post-Cash children for baptism at St Bartholomew's, suffered the phrase 'living in adultery' in the 1869 entry in the Baptism Book. Amelia had little time for the establishment, turned away from the Established Church and became a keen supporter of the 'more democratic' Mission Church which, on Mill Lane, was within earshot of St Bartholomew's. Her death in 1925 was followed by that of the minister in 1927, whereupon the borrowed iron building was dismantled and removed. She was a great asset to the local community and much loved by family and neighbours. She was also the first literate member of the Burgess family.

The first child of Andrew and Amelia, Bertha Burgess (1883-1968), was born three years after the marriage. A girl and two boys followed, all leaving home on marriage. Two later children, Samuel and Elizabeth Amelia, both died in the 1890s at a few months old.

Teenage girls who disliked the idea of working at Greg's or going into domestic service (also anathema to the Burgesses) had a slightly more palatable alternative – Fustian cutting and velvet dividing at Dearden's on Manchester Road – of which Amelia had already had experience. It was situated close to home, but, at the same time, was an unhealthy and boring job with depressing wages. Bertha, who started at fourteen on leaving Chancel Lane School, received only a few shillings a week and hated it. This only left Greg's – what would great grandfather have said?

She started work in Greg's winding section in March 1900 as one of 187 workers, and brought home 8s 4½d at the end of the week. She hoped it would not be for long, for she had met Joseph Acton (1880-1955), a journey-man bricklayer. He was from another old Wilmslow family which, like the Burgesses, had marriage links with the Moores. Also like the Burgess', the Acton's had shown no interest in millwork, being heavily involved in brickmaking and bricklaying. Thomas Acton (1834-1903) of Bollin Walk and Bollin Hill became a brickmaker-employer – the only excursion by the Burgess' and Acton's into the higher levels of capitalism before 1930.

Joseph Acton was born on Manchester Road, across from Dearden's cutting rooms where his mother Elizabeth (née Worth) and his future wife had both worked. In 1902 he was working on mill chimneys in Stockport and lodging near the centre of town. He married Bertha Burgess later that year. With the birth of their first child, Frederick, in August 1903, the family moved to a rented house in Lowndes Lane, Stockport. Although Joseph advertised his trade in the Stockport Directory of 1905, the family returned to Wilmslow and settled in a small cottage in Mount Pleasant (Lacey Green). Bertha's work at the mill was disrupted therefore by journeys to Stockport, house moving and pregnancy. Nevertheless, in her completed weeks as a winder she brought home an invaluable ten or eleven shillings. Seeing Joseph obtain regular work as a bricklayer in Wilmslow, Bertha left Greg's and determined that her boy would go into the building trade. True, there was no pay in bad weather – indeed there was a big temptation to gamble earlier pay on the horses or on card games played on wet or frosty days when the 'brickies' were marooned in their hut. Still,

Joseph brought his money home – as long as he had a quiet life and enough spare money to grow prize chrysanthemums and tomatoes and to breed racing pigeons (another potential source of gambling that had to be controlled). Bertha felt bricklaying gave some sort of independence – an old craft selling a valuable service. Great grandfather would have approved.

Bertha was a strong Liberal before and after gaining the vote in 1918. Every day she avidly read the non-Tory press and was proud of her non-conformist or ronter ('ranter') upbringing under Amelia. She was markedly anti-socialist and anti-big business; but she was a keen supporter of the monarchy.

The Fist World War brought both a local slump in the building trade and a period of

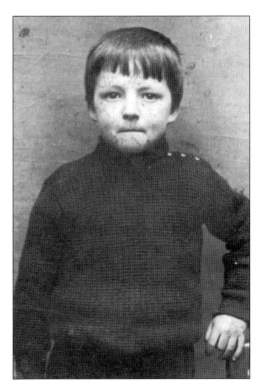

*Frederick Acton (1903-1975) aged five years, at Chancel Lane School, Wilmslow.*

sharp inflation which forced her back to Greg's in 1915 when her youngest son Joseph was four and the middle boy, Andrew, still had to do two years at Chancel Lane School, Frederick, however, was leaving the school in the summer, and in her mind, he was still destined for the building trade. In his mind, on the other hand, he was intended to be a Northrop loom operator. Some wages at Greg's had nearly doubled since 1914; the husband of Bertha's sister, a loom jobber, had reached 24/- a week and as early as 1916 some women weavers were taking home 23/-. Bertha decided to take Frederick with her. Building would pick up after the war and

Freddie would be apprenticed to a master builder – despite his protestations about the cold, the rain and wage-less days. He could join his father and his father's father and get into a freer, assured and more manly occupation:

'The boy mulled over the woman's remark and recognised she was trying to cheer him up. Once they turned off Styal Road, something approaching confidence returned. An office man told him where to report for twist drawing. The woman took him and left him and hurried to her winding job. Although by 5.30 p.m. he had not managed to operate a Northrop, the boy was cheered by the thought of 10/- at the end of the week. He would soon move up to weaving. That evening, he led the way home; he had found the right career at the first go.'

He was right, for a while. In August 1919 he moved up to the Northrops at over 27/- a week. By May 1920 he reached 60/-, his mother 35/-. With his father's 30/- and Andrew soon to start work, the family made real gains. But mill wages began to fall in the later months of 1920. In no time at all, Frederick at seventeen was apprenticed to a master bricklayer. By 1930, the mill's business was collapsing. Frederick, now thoroughly happy in his second career, was a master builder employing six men and managing things his way. Perhaps great, great grandfather Robert Burgess Senior was happy at last.

*Ray Acton*

*Frederick Acton with his father Joseph, showing off racing pigeons, c. 1925.*

*Frederick Acton, son of Bertha and Joseph, in his mid-teens, working at Greg's.*

# 3  Societies, Institutions and Charities

## Wilmslow Guild – independent centre for adult education

*Origins*

Soon after the First World War Maud and Russell Brayshaw moved house, from South Manchester to a home in Dean Row, Wilmslow. Russell, twelve years older than Maud, had an engineering business in east Manchester. They were not strangers to Wilmslow for they had previously, and for some years, taken a home in the area, and being Quakers they soon became members of the Morley Meeting at its large house on the corner of Altrincham Road and Bourne Street. At that time Bourne Street was virtually the west boundary of the town; it was built up only as far as Simpson Street. Russell's education – he was born in 1879 – was largely self-acquired through reading, adult schools, concert and theatre going. Maud particularly shared his interests in drama and music, and their house became a focus for play-readings, recitals and discussions. They were to live in Wilmslow for thirty-eight years, a significant time for the development of the Wilmslow Guild.

At that time a number of adult education classes were running in the town, run by various churches and the Wilmslow Educational Association, with links to Manchester University tutorial classes and the Workers Educational Association. Evening classes and lectures were held in private houses, schools, church premises and the British Workman Mission Hall on Grove Street. Maud Brayshaw realised the value of the little-used Quaker Schoolroom adjacent to the Meeting House above the carriage shed and stables, and from 1923 it was used for groups that could no longer be accommodated in private houses, though always subject to agreement with the Friends and a charge.

The Brayshaw's were influenced by the Educational Settlements Association, established in 1920 under the leadership of Arnold Rowntree, the York Quaker. Settlements were administered by a paid warden and run by their own members; they were described as 'institutions created by the socially and educationally privileged for the benefit of the unprivileged'. While this might have been in some part true in Wilmslow, given the social standing of the begetters of the Wilmslow Educational Association the circumstances there were vastly different from those in the inner urban locations of other settlements such as Leeds and Birkenhead – Wilmslow offered a different field for ploughing.

By April 1926, with this background in mind, there was a division in the approaches to adult education in the town. More formal classes and lectures continued under the Association, generally on more vocational lines, but the Wilmslow Beacon Guild was founded separately:

'to establish a Community Centre at which men and women may find opportunities for the enrichment of life through education, fellowship and cooperative effort for the welfare of the community...open to all men and women without distinction of class, party or creed.'

What foresight! Although the concept of 'community' may have changed over the decades, these forward-looking objectives were to provide continuity that has survived beyond three quarters of a century in Wilmslow Guild, supported by a succession of paid wardens (now Head of Centre) and, through the decades, hosts of volunteer member-helpers and elected committees. One of only four or five independent centres in the country surviving from the 1920s, the Guild owes its long-lived strength both to the loyalty and ability of its members and to the continuing affluence of its environment.

*Early Years*

In thirteen years the Beacon Guild blossomed into a vigorous society of over 500 members, with a multitude of activities including a Campers' Club ('tents available'), a Ramblers' Club and a Women's Hockey Club, as well as language classes (French, German, Italian and English). The Citizenship Group discussed social and political topics, which grew increasingly significant as war loomed in the 1930s. The

*Front of the Guild Syllabus for 1942/43. (Courtesy the Wilmslow Guild)*

Arts Group included both painting and crafts, as well as drama – ever favourite with Maud Brayshaw; in its first year the Drama Group, whose only previous experience was in one-act plays, staged an ambitious Shakespeare – King John. This was the beginning of the Guild Players, still one of the town's leading drama groups, where learning stagecraft and production are as important as acting.

At that time most women's lives were homebound. The Women's Group at the Guild began to widen horizons, with discussions and talks on health and social matters, childcare, family planning and literature as well as entertainment and crafts.

*Making hats in the hut, 1949. (Courtesy the Wilmslow Guild)*

This Group became the workhouse of the Guild, providing the ideas and labour for the Players' wardrobe making, fund raising, and running the canteen in the Common Room, amongst many other functions. Through the decades it has numbered hundreds of women too numerous to mention, whose input to the Guild has been just as important as that of the men who can be named as its 'leaders'.

With wartime, activities became more focused but still widely social and educational. The Warden, Ruth Macdonald, a young graduate, had to resign as the Guild's finances were unlikely to support her; she could not then have known that she would come back some forty years later, as Dr Ruth Cowhig, a very popular tutor in literature, teaching for another twenty years. One of the members, an indomitable lady called Ruth Stillitoe, was persuaded to undertake the warden's duties; she also tutored in French language. Mrs Stillitoe maintained her service until 1943, even after a road accident three years earlier resulted in the amputation of a leg below the knee – she had been cycling back from the Brayshaw's. Six months later, she was back at her duties.

Food and coal rationing constrained the social activities of the Common Room (it only had a coal fire for heating) and blackout restrictions enforced changes in other functions. The Women's Group started a Knitting Group as part of the national effort. The members' subscription, 6d. since the beginning, was raised to one shilling, and the name was changed to Wilmslow Guild.

In these years the Guild had only the schoolroom as well as the use of a section of the Meeting House as a common room, furnished with begged and borrowed furniture, and a small room for the warden, who used a borrowed typewriter; the purchase of a second-hand machine for £2 10s. was a major financial decision. The schoolroom, though large, was undivided, so multiple simultaneous use was difficult – but it suited the Guild Players very well. It also gave a home to the Unnamed Society, a drama group bombed out of their home in Salford – periodically providing a 'home' to other organizations in need of temporary help – such help remained typical of the Guild's community spirit.

One wartime innovation which later benefited the Guild was the construction at the lower end of the paddock, behind the Meeting House, of a hut. Constructed by the Ministry of Defence it was intended to receive evacuees, but appears not to have been needed for this purpose. After the war, the Society of Friends (with Maud Bradshaw's persuasion) succeeded in securing its use by the Guild, thereby greatly increasing the space available for activities, even though it had no heating or water laid on. This allowed rapid expansion of the Syllabus.

*The Modern Years – and a building*

By mid-century, with 1930s and post-war housing development, Wilmslow had already expanded, bringing in newcomers to live on the Pownall estates and elsewhere, and demand for Guild activities grew accordingly. All efforts were now bent towards providing new accommodation for classes, courses and meetings, which required substantial fund-raising as well as seeking grants. Hilda Band, involved in Guild affairs since its early years, was elected to organize the building fund in 1957, and with tremendous help from the membership the Guild's own building was opened in 1963 (with 1,300 members), and was extended in 1972. It was constructed on the paddock behind the Meeting House, with access from Bourne Street. The Guild Players could now adapt the Quaker schoolroom as a small theatre.

Hilda Band, Vice Chairman or Chairman from 1969 to 1978, remained an active member until the end of the century, her last class being Chinese Embroidery. The building as it stands today now offers classes, courses and group activities to some 2,500 members each year. Although it is still associated with the Educational Centres Association (successor to Educational Settlements Association) it is a far cry from those original adult centres and from the Adult Schools of Russell Brayshaw's youth. Some activities draw members from addresses far outside the Wilmslow community, and there is great competition for places on many of the courses.

*The pottery room at the Guild, 1976. (Courtesy the Wilmslow Guild)*

*The people who make it work*

All this is made possible only by devoted volunteer effort. Enrolment week is a marvel of organization – and a highly social occasion – devised originally by Hilda Band and later administered by Nora Curtis, with an extensive body of helpers throughout the week. The office is manned daily throughout each annual session by a roster of members, and various committees are responsible for the ongoing management. The programmes of the several Groups are planned and administered by their own committees, answering to the Guild's Executive Committee.

The Convener of the Syllabus Committee is John Spawton, Head of Centre since 1984. This elected committee plans the programme annually, ready for distribution each July to members and a wide range of libraries and other places. In this work the Assistant Head, Joan Platt, is assisted by several other volunteers.

While the Guild has no permanent teaching staff, it has long drawn on many highly qualified tutors and lecturers, such as Peter McLoughlin, tutor in English Folk Dancing from 1960 to 1998; Annwen Nicholas (Creative Embroidery) and Barbara Mencel (Chinese and Traditional Embroidery) who both started teaching in 1978 and have developed their fields until the present day; Fred Broadhurst, a young geology lecturer on a Manchester University Extension course in 1955, who has in recent decades developed a field study course for the Guild as far away as Hawaii. These are but a few of very many popular

*Painting class at the Guild, 1976. (Courtesy Wilmslow Guild)*

tutors, constantly developing courses in many fields – no wonder there is such a demand at enrolment time.

### 'Electing the right man'

In her ten-year history of the Beacon Guild (1936) Maud Brayshaw wrote 'As so often has happened in the Guild's history, the right man appeared at a critical moment'. This could have been remarked at many times in subsequent years, as a succession of officers have served it. All the Chairmen but Hilda Band (1975 to 1978) have been men, many of them in professions – and most of them vigorously involved in the Guild Players! Many served as Vice-Chairmen before taking full office. It was usually the case that their wives were also involved in Guild service of some kind. There is space

here to mention only some of the individuals who have guided the Guild's fortunes.

Russell Brayshaw, the first Chairman, served for thirteen years up to the outbreak of war, though he had many other public commitments. His Honorary Treasurer was Harold F. Clarke, one of the original group which initiated the Guild, who also served until 1939. His wife led the first band of designers and sewers for the wardrobe of stage costumes. Another founder member, Allan Martindale, served as a Secretary or Treasurer until 1940. This man was typical of the Guild's workers: a Rating Officer in local government, he was also an organizer in the National Savings Movement, Honorary Librarian of Alderley Edge branch library, served at the Methodist

# "PEER GYNT"

## *Characters in order of their appearance.*

| | |
|---|---|
| ASE, a peasant's widow, Peer's mother ...... | JESSIE BURMAN. |
| PEER GYNT (in Part 1.) ...... ...... | DERWENT BRAYSHAW |
| KARI, Ase's neighbour ...... ...... ...... | GWEN ANDREW |
| THE FARMER at HEGSTAD, Ingrid's father | HARRY GOODACRE |
| THE BRIDEGROOM, ...... ...... | ALLAN MARTINDALE |
| BRIDEGROOM'S FATHER ...... | GRAHAM SCOTT |
| BRIDEGROOM'S MOTHER ...... ...... | RUTH SILLITOE |
| AN OLD PEASANT ...... ...... | ROY WATERS |
| A FIDDLER ...... ...... ...... | BEATRICE LYTHGOE |
| ASLAK, a smith ...... ...... | ARTHUR WALPOLE |

PEASANTS— E. METCALFE, M. BRAYSHAW, F. EVANS, E. WRIGLEY,
E. ASHLEY-TAYLOR, A. PROCTER, D. PLANT, M. FERGUSSON, M. RYE,
K. GLANCEY, D. STEVENS, E. GRIPPER, R. ROBERTS, I. WATERS, A. HOLT.

| | |
|---|---|
| SOLVEIG ...... ...... ...... ...... | GRETA JAFFREY |
| SOLVEIG'S FATHER ...... ...... | RUPERT KAY |
| SOLVEIG'S MOTHER ...... ...... | HANNAH WORTHINGTON |
| HELGA, Solveig's sister ...... ...... | ESTER RAMSKILL |
| INGRID, the bride ...... ...... | MONA JONES |
| A GREEN-CLAD WOMAN, the Troll King's daughter | EVA MARSDEN |
| THE KING OF THE TROLLS ...... ...... | WILLIAM OUGHTRED |
| THE TROLL-CHAMBERLAIN ...... ...... | MARTYN BRAYSHAW |
| A DANCING TROLL ...... ...... ...... | RUTH ROBERTS |

TROLLS & IMPS— C. PAINE, M. KAY, M. ROGERS, R. WATERS,
I. WATERS, E. METCALFE, E. WRIGLEY, E. ASHLEY-TAYLOR, A. PROCTER,
D. PLANT, M. FERGUSSON, M. RYE, K. GLANCEY, D. STEVENS, A. HOLT,
A. MARTINDALE, G. SCOTT. A. WALPOLE, J. EMERSON, M. BRELAND,
C. WARBURTON, M. LUDLAM, D. BROUGHTON, G. MIDDLETON,
A. OPENSHAW,

| | |
|---|---|
| PEER GYNT (in parts 2 & 3.) ...... ...... | ERIC BARBER |
| HERR VON EBERKOPF ...... ...... | CLIFFORD PAINE |
| Mr. COTTON ...... ...... | ARTHUR WALPOLE |
| MONSIEUR BALLON ...... ...... | WILLIAM OUGHTRED |
| A MOROCCAN SERVANT ...... | MARTYN BRAYSHAW |
| A VILLAGE PASTOR ...... ...... | CLIFFORD PAINE |
| A BUTTON MOULDER ...... ...... | MAURICE ROGERS |
| A LEAN PERSON (The Devil) ...... | J. B. SMITH |

## THE PLAY produced by ERIC BARBER.

| | |
|---|---|
| Assistant Producer: ...... ...... | MAUDE BRAYSHAW |
| Stage Management & Scenery Construction : ...... | JAMES SIMPSON |
| | and ROY WATERS |
| Properties : ...... ...... ...... | GWEN PORTER |
| Curtain Bearers : HAROLD DODSON, MICHAEL STOCKTON, |
| | JOHN EVANS. |

*Cast list for the 1940 production of* Peer Gynt. *Ray Waters is credited for Stage Management and Scenery Production. (Courtesy Wilmslow Guild)*

Church, Water Lane – and represented the Guild on the local branch of the League of nations Union, was a Guild Player and played badminton. His obituary in the Alderley Edge and Wilmslow Advertiser, 24 August 1945, read 'he was salt of the earth. He never minded playing that most difficult instrument in life's orchestra: second fiddle.' Brayshaw was succeeded as Chairman by Bill Oughtred, a timber merchant and a dapper individual, who also liked to strut the stage.

The establishment of ICI Research Laboratories at Alderley Park in the early 1940s brought an influx of new residents who quickly took advantage of what the Guild had to offer, commonly the fun and pleasure of being Guild Players. They soon took an interest in Guild management. Clifford Pain, Chairman from 1946 to 1955, was an extrovert member of the Players, before leaving to take up a new ICI appointment in London; his wife, Phyllis Paine, was joint Treasurer from 1945 to 1955, and amongst other commitments, designed costumes for the Players. His place was taken by another ICI man, Vice-Chairman Dr Ronald Martin. Between 1944 and 1949, a pioneer pharmaceutical scientist, Arthur Walpole, was the Guild

*Arthur Walpole, 'Walop' (left) in* Old Man of the Mountains *– 1952. (Courtesy Wilmslow Guild)*

*Celebrating the Guild's 50th Anniversary. Back row: George Band, J. Herwald Morris (Mayor), Frank Brooks, Hilda Band, Edith Lyle, Julian Noble, David Brayshaw. Front row: Maud Brayshaw, D. Hunter, Christine Fowler. Courtesy Wilmslow Guild.*

Secretary and an ardent Guild Player. Affectionately known as 'Walop', in his profession he was credited with the discovery of Tamoxifen and its subsequent application as an anti-cancer agent.

Dr Ben Collie, also an 'ICI man', took over as Chairman between 1958 and 1961 and later served as Treasurer until 1978, the period in which the new building was planned and financed; he significantly contributed to the Guild's financial welfare. His wife Myra Collie was another mainstay of Guild organization, and represented it at the Old People's Welfare Association. After their deaths, their estates generously benefited the Guild.

In 1939 Roy and Ivy Waters came out to visit their old school friend, Ron Martin and his wife; they also enjoyed a performance of Twelfth Night (produced by Paine and Oughtred, stage managed by Martin), liking the place so much that they very shortly moved from Crumpsall to Wilmslow – even though this meant that Roy had to commute to his work at ICI Blackley. Within a year they were both playing peasants and producing scenery for open-air performances of *Peer Gynt*. Both continue a vigorous participation in Guild activities. Ivy and her daughter Janet Douglas (a pillar of the Guild Players) are the finance queens of Enrolment Week, keeping the books balance day by day.

In 1964 Frank Brooks became Chairman for two years, then again from 1969 to 1975 and 1983 to 1991. He was of a different mould to the ICI men – he described himself as 'a village lad;. At age fourteen, in 1932, his immediate act on leaving school was to join the junior section of the Guild, to fulfil his ardent ambitions in amateur acting. Throughout his life, apart from during war service in the Army, he took part in most aspects of Guild work. After he married, his wife Edna joined the Women's Group. He once remarked that the Guild had progressed from the days of social class distinction to the broader social structure of today. Certainly the original aim of the Settlements to educate the 'unprivileged' has long been superseded here.

Succeeding Frank Brooks as Chairman came Geoffrey Reed, yet another Guild Player of long standing, serving from 1991 to 2002. Like so many of his predecessors he brought professional training to benefit the Guild – and his wife, Grace, another devotee of the dramatic art, has continued the long development of the costume collection as Wardrobe Mistress, both designing and sewing. In the last decade they have produced between them – with help from others – vast ranges of scenery and clothing. But the Guild Players continually renew themselves – younger adherents administer and sustain this vital part of the Guild's history.

Geoffrey Reed's term of office has been part of a triumvirate with Stan Marsden working as an astute Treasurer (again calling on his professional experience) and Margaret Norton as Secretary. She had the longest Guild history of the three, having joined a Scottish Dancing Class in the wartime hut in the early 1950s, progressing through Soft Furnishing classes and others to assist in the organisation of the Theatre Club and the Music and Concert Club, and very significantly on the House Committee – very important; someone has to keep the roof over the Guild's head in good fettle.

Margaret Morton was one in a succession of women Secretaries since 1969, a sign of the changing role of women in our society. Marjorie Robinson, Jane Betts and Joan Brown preceded her, all for lengthy and onerous periods, and Shelagh Vernon Smith has succeeded her. Jill Dodson and Della Williams served as Treasurers, also for several years.

And what of the first woman in the Guild's history? Both Maud and Russell Brayshaw undertook heavy commitments at national level in the Society of Friends as years went on. They left Wilmslow in 1958 to live in the Lake District, having bequeathed to the town an idea that has benefited thousands of individuals in developing their own lives. In 1936 Maud pictured the ten-year-old Guild as an acorn that had fed on its environment to grow into an admirable young tree – 'a living, growing organism'. She wrote:

'If ever the willingness to experiment and take risks dies out of the Guild and it settles into a rut; if its members are content to come to it merely for what they can get; if it becomes a resort of comfortable cliques of people who all know each other and don't want outsiders then, though the tree may continue to flourish in outward appearance for some time, it will have begun to die.'

A long succession of members of the Wilmslow Guild seem to have been able to ensure that her tree would be kept living and healthy. A far-seeing woman, she was able to see it reach good maturity; she died in 1992, just short of her 102nd birthday.

*Marguerita Oughton*

57

*Wilmslow Guild Players 2002 production of* Garlic and Lavender, *a vampire spoof. From left to right: Ruth O'Hara, Bill Beton, Toby Jones, Tracey Jarrett. (Courtesy Bill Beton)*

## Early memories of the Guild

Although my first views of the Guild were in the 1950s when I attended Wilmslow Meeting with my future husband and in-laws – the O'Brien family, it was not until we moved to Alderley Edge in 1970 that I joined any of the activities. Even so I was aware that the Wilmslow Guild was highly regarded as a mecca of further education, and that many of the Wilmslow Friends were involved in the varied activities.

Denis and I eagerly attended several classes either individually or together when 'children-sitting' could be arranged. I well remember a Geology class that kept us spellbound, the

lecturer enthusiastically expounded the early theories of 'Tectonics' – the plate movement of the Earth's surface. He presented the early proofs so clearly that he soon convinced us lay people that it was a valid theory! It came as no surprise to me to find it was an established fact, when I was getting my Open University degree many years later. Nevertheless, Denis and I felt we were discovering 'earth-moving' new facts of life!

The Christmas fairs were interesting events – in fact they could be described as forerunners to the 'craft fairs' so popular nowadays.

One valued present to come from the Guild was a bright orange, velvet, bridge table cover, that's still in use. Margery Spendlow had it made especially for us to enliven our 'autumn tinted' lounge and to protect a lovely old mahogany table bought for thirty-five shillings from a local auction. Those were the days!

I believe Marjory Spendlow was one of the earliest Wardrobe Mistresses and I well remember Sunday teas with her and her mother, Jessie Bruce, finding them repairing some of the costumes.

Remembered with affection were the country walks with Julian Noble, particularly one in Lyme Park. We had been quietly observing deer rutting and were much amused after a fight between two magnificent stags, to see the younger, defeated stag trot nonchalantly off to be followed immediately by a little doe – it absolutely made the day for my children.

When Denis and I left Chester we had to change from the Scottish dancing we had been involved in there to English country dancing at the Guild, but we quickly made friends and had many happy Monday nights – and even happier open nights when our refreshments were greatly appreciated, and brought people from quite a distance.

For one of the Jubilee celebrations (and after much persuasion) we all dressed up and paraded in the streets of Wilmslow; after overcoming our initial embarrassment we quite enjoyed ourselves. I wonder if our Guild members would do this now?

*Joyce O'Brien*

# Soroptomist International of Wilmslow and District

In 1968 a group of ladies living in and around Wilmslow got together to form the Wilmslow Soroptomists. Some local residents when they first heard the name thought that this was to be a Concert Party! Soroptimism, however, is an international organization for women in management and the professions working through service projects to advance human rights and the status of women.

The first meeting was held on Tuesday 14 May at the Royal School for the Deaf, and Miss Isabel McWilliam, who was Governor of Styal Women's Prison and the prime mover in getting the club started, was elected as the first President.

At the top of the agenda for the first meeting of the Executive Committee was 'Meetings – where and when?' A great number of venues were suggested; mostly local pubs or hotels, and prices seemed to range from 7/6d to 2 guineas. The Cherry's Hotel (now the County) on Alderley Road was the popular choice, but as it wasn't available until September, Miss Kinsey, who was headmistress of St Hilary's, offered a room at the school until then. The Annual Subscription for membership was set at 4 guineas with an entrance fee of 2 guineas. The club wasn't, however, able to meet at the Cherry's, and meetings continued to be held at St Hilary's, or in members' houses, until 1969, when a permanent home for fortnightly meetings was found at the Bowling Club in Knutsford Road, with quarterly dinners to be held at the Stanneylands Hotel.

Much thought was give to the design of a badge of office for the President. A Miss Cartwright was asked to produce a design, and after due deliberation it was decided to incorporate Wilmslow Parish church, the Cheshire wheat sheaves, the Wizard of Alderley Edge and his white horse, with the River Bollin running through the whole. It was to include the Soroptomist motto

Above: *Soroptomists Charter Dinner, 1968. From left to right: Mayor H. Thornburn, Miss C. Evans, Mrs H. Thornburn, Miss I.M. McWilliam, Mrs M.E. Denham, Mr P. Dronsfeld, Mrs P. Dronsfeld.*

*Soroptomists Presidents Badge.*

'Looking Further', and be surrounded by the full name of the club. The badge was made by a local jeweller in silver gilt with the picture in enamel. This resulted in a very beautiful badge which has been worn with much pride by successive Presidents ever since.

The Charter Dinner was held at the Belfry Hotel on Tuesday 26 November, 1968. The Charter was presented to the Wilmslow Founder President by the President of the Soroptomist International of Great Britain and Northern Ireland. A number of local dignitaries were present, including Cllr Peter Dronsfield (Chairman of Wilmslow Council) and his wife, Cllr Thornburn (Chairman of Alderley Edge Council) and his wife, Canon and Mrs Reeman and Mr Woolley (President of Wilmslow and Alderley Edge Rotary Club) and his wife. In addition to the Federation President and the Divisional Union President there were officers and members present from many neighbouring Soroptomist Clubs.

The format for meetings was much the same as it is now, with them being held on the second and fourth Tuesdays in the month, one to be a business meeting and one a speaker meeting. One of the speakers in 1969 was Dr Simon Freeman, who spoke on drug dependency. This is a subject that has been discussed, studied, and reported on at Club level, regionally and internationally ever since.

From the beginning the President stressed the service aspect of Soroptimism, and the necessity for the Club to become involved with, and help, the local community. Over the years members have been involved in a number of local projects, from telephone calls and parcels at Christmas for the housebound, to tea-bars at the Mary Dendy Hospital and Styal Prison. The CAB, the CVS, Crossroads Caring for Carers and the Hospices, have all benefited. However, such projects not only need hands-on help, but also money.

The first charity event in October 1968 was a 'Chapeau et Chignons' show, where members acted as models. This raised £50, which was sent to Shelter. This was followed by the usual jumble sales, coffee mornings, and more fashion shows. In 1974 the first number of very successful art exhibitions was organized. The first one was opened by Miss Helen Bradley, a well-known artist who lived in Wilmslow. The following year the exhibition was opened by Miss Eileen Derbyshire (Emily Bishop of Coronation Street).

An important aspect of Soroptimism is it's internationalism. The first visit to a Federation Annual Conference was made in 1973, when the Wilmslow Club President travelled to Sydney, Australia. Since then many such trips have been made and visitors from overseas entertained here. A friendship link with Cambrai in France, has resulted in numerous visits and parties on both sides of the Channel, and built many lasting friendships – I know my husband will never forget being kissed on both cheeks by a Frenchman on Wilmslow Station, fortunately his blushes were spared as the station was almost deserted! Entertaining overseas visitors has figured largely in the Club's social calendar throughout the years. On one memorable occasion when some overseas students at Manchester University were coming to have tea in Alderley Edge, it started to snow very heavily. We donned our Wellingtons and layers of clothing to meet our visitors at the station, and escort them safely through the increasingly deep snow to a member's home in London Road. The students were African and had never seen snow before, and were very surprised at how wet it made them. When we arrived at our destination there was a lovely coal fire burning in the grate – again this was a first, as they had never seen a fire burning indoors before, and this became the highlight of their visit.

Soroptimism is a forward-looking organization which is very relevant to the twenty-first century, but when reading the early records and minutes of past meetings I have come to realise how little has needed to change. Obviously the size of the subscriptions and the amount of money needed for charitable projects has increased enormously, but the aims and objectives remain the same – to strive for the advancement of the status of women, high ethical standards and human rights for all – and we are still committed to service local, national and international communities.

Modern methods of communication have revolutionised contacts with other Soroptimists at all levels, and the Wilmslow Club is finding e-mail particularly useful for keeping in touch with a friend at the Harare Club.

Throughout the last thirty-four years, the members of the Club have still found time to organize parties and enjoy themselves. This year it is the Queen's Golden Jubilee and we are going to share this ability with as many members of the public as possible. We are holding a giant street party in Grove Street on Monday 26 August 2002. We hope people will enjoy it and help us to raise money for the David Lewis Centre – Soroptimists will continue 'looking further'.

*Mrs Monica Raffle – a member of the Wilmslow Club since 1972.*

## Lamb Soup, Green Shield Stamps and Carpet Rolls

My contribution to the history of Wilmslow concerns a modest corner of the town and a relatively recent period, that is the twenty-five years during which CVS has operated in the town. CVS is the abbreviated name, which in full is the Council for Voluntary Service, and this article is an abbreviated version of our history. The three assorted items in the title are all bit-players in the story.

Right from the start – in case you spot a certain partiality and possessiveness about the way CVS is described – I have to declare an interest. I have worked for CVS in Wilmslow for twelve years now, almost half its life here in the town. As you can imagine, I feel a real attachment to it. A second fact which I need to point out, which may well colour this picture, is that the organization is currently at a crucial turning point in its history. Whatever the future turns out to be the CVS in Wilmslow will never look the same again, not least because we have just had to move out of the building which has been our home since 1976.

The story I wish to tell begins, for the sake of this piece, in the early 1970s. Macclesfield already had a CVS then, and there was encouragement both from them and from the local community in Wilmslow to try to set up something locally. A number of groups in the voluntary sector supported the idea, as well as Macclesfield Borough Council and the Social Services department of Cheshire County Council; it was from the latter two bodies, as well as the public, that funds were raised to begin to make this possible. By the time of the first AGM in May 1976, there was an established committee and the first paid worker had been appointed. Mrs Anne Cobb was minuted as having been in post for two months. Initially, with no independent office from which to work, she was based within Social Services.

*The Advertiser* newspaper in Wilmslow ran a piece about CVS that autumn. It publicised the official opening of the first office for the Wilmslow CVS, in October 1976, and explained that 'the aims of the local branch are to discover the needs within the community, focus public attention on those needs and organize local community resources'. CVS has gone on making itself aware of government initiatives, local services, and gaps in provision, and looking out for the most important resource to make community action possible – that is, volunteers.

The first office, so I am told, had been a small butcher's shop and dairy, off Water Lane, to the side of the Co-Op (now Thomas Cook's). It was in a poor state, with a powerful unpleasant smell and needed a thorough cleaning; blood had to be scrubbed off the walls! Volunteers rallied to help.

Within a year, there were changes. A new Voluntary Services Organiser was appointed, Caroline Melliar-Smith, and a new home had been found which would give CVS more space and an improved identity. The office moved to a terraced house at 33 Manchester Road, which has been its home ever since. Cheshire County Council offered the property as an office, though the building was classified as being not suitable for domestic use; gradually work had to be done to improve the décor and facilities. Once again, volunteers were found to help. The new office still lacked certain refinements. For a time, kettles of water had to be fetched from across the road to make

drinks. And calor gas stoves were brought in to provide heating – except that they turned the air into a total fug, as staff recall. It would be several years (1987) before storage heaters were installed. In 1982, it was recorded (with some pride, it seems) that the office had remained open 'throughout the severe winter weather [with the] office temperature 56 degrees and below, despite burst pipes'.

As early as 1982, Cheshire County Council surveyed the premises in Manchester Road and raised concerns about safety, especially with regard to the top floor of the three-storey building. The building was rewired as a result of the visit, and life went on as normal. Work was done (by volunteers) to improve the kitchen and toilet area in 1983, and the peppercorn rent paid by CVS to the County Council was increased. In 1986, the office received a donation from Marks & Spencer of carpeting taken up during shop refitting. By 1989, the Chairman reported to the AGM on recent work 'to renovate our premises – the exterior is a joy to behold, the main offices are fresh and bright, [and] new floor coverings adorn the kitchen and upstairs front room'.

In spite of this cosmetic make-over, the branch secretary had to report during the next year that the County Council had inspected the building once again, and had found it 'surplus to requirements and its sale was being considered'. Things did not look good. Not much more was heard, however, till 1999 when another survey was done and report made; the forecast was definitely not encouraging. The building was in a poor structural state and it was suggested that around £30,000 was needed to make it good. Neither CVS nor CCC were in a position to fund such repairs. The final blow came at the beginning of July 2002 when CVS sought to renew insurance cover for staff and other users of the offices, only to be told that the risks were too great. Everyone was advised to move out at once.

It might have been a fate we had seen approaching, but, as with many of life's blows, this *coup de grace* was shocking news. Notices went up in the window the same day to announce that the building was closed. Power was switched off and telephone calls re-routed. The Wilmslow Express newspaper ran a front-page feature about CVS, including a photograph of the notice of closure and headlined 'Volunteers Homeless'. Within a week or two the building inside began to smell musty and abandoned.

As I write this piece, CVS has been given asylum for a few weeks at the Wilmslow Guild, who have very generously taken us in. For the longer term, we wait to see. Discussions will be held, help sought, and kind offers considered. All we know is that the current arrangement – whereby staff and volunteers are sharing a Guild lecture room with rolls of carpet and scenery on its summer break from the Guild Players storage rooms – is just a temporary reprieve.

The building, of course, is only a part of CVS's history in Wilmslow and only a minor landmark in the geography of Manchester Road. It has nevertheless been a part of Wilmslow's identity for a quarter of a century as home to CVS. In its time I am told it was a sweet shop for a while, and before that, perhaps, part of the industrial heritage of the town, associated with the textile mills and finishing processes which occupied several sites near to the Bollin and on the Manchester Road. A guess suggests the building may be as much as 200 years old, as are other properties further up the hill, constructed on land leased for building in 1792. The short, wide internal doorways are one of the only original features, belonging to a distant past that can now only be imagined.

The building has been an outward and visible sign of CVS is Wilmslow. There is much more that needs recording, not least the organization's involvement in community events and concerns. Over the years, there has been commitment from a wide range of local agencies and volunteers, who have brought in their enthusiasm and ideas. Members of the committees have discussed unemployment and disability awareness issues, helped run a youth event and held surveys on various areas of the town, looking at wasys in which services could help improve things for people.

As a result, new services have been developed, including the office becoming a distribution point for hearing-aid batteries. In 1990/91, for instance, it is recorded that the office had had 380 callers to enquire about or collect batteries. Several other schemes were set up, for example, to involve people with sight impairment as visitors at Styal Prison, or to run sewing groups, or organize befriending of older people. One of the busiest projects was running and manning the community car scheme, through which volunteers offered transport to those in need. Eventually, through fund raising efforts and donations from Round Table and Help the Aged, sufficient money was raised to buy a twelve-seat Renault minibus, with tail lift, which was bought in 1985 for £7,638. Not only did the bus improve transport facilities, but it starred in several Wilmslow events, adorned with posters and paper flowers; there are photographs of it in processions and at the Carnival which used to be held on the Carrs in the 1980s. In 1989, Community

Transport Macclesfield Borough was set up and the service became a district-wide provision.

Other schemes came along. CVS supported setting up local furniture recycling projects, with the Wilmslow area Furniture Phone Line being established and registered as a charity in its own right in 1992. People got involved in the planning and establishment of the Wilmslow Talking Newspaper, which ran initially at Lindow School (from 1983). CVS ran Christmas toy schemes (and still does), to redirect gifts from the public to families in need, and raised funds to enable deprived local children to go on holidays. Bereavement support work began. CVS joined in on discussions around setting up East Cheshire Hospice and a scheme to enable disabled young people to access leisure activities; it was involved in helping found the Wilmslow Area Accommodation Project. It grappled with the implications of Care in the Community legislation and supported a campaign to raise awareness of access issues to public places, and more.

In the early 1980s CVS provided office space for the organizers of the government Manpower Services Commission schemes, through which work such as decorating and gardening was done. By October 1982, 230 jobs had been tackled; in June 1985 it was reported that seventy people were involved in this work. The closure of the Commission in 1988 brought this very valuable community work to an end – though people in touch with CVS still refer back to the 'once upon a time' when there were ways of providing help with gardening and decorating.

Over the years, some of the groups with which CVS was working came to share the Manchester Road premises. At various times probation services have used rooms, and Marriage Guidance. WRVS had its local office there for many years, and Talking Newspaper moved in for a time. Barnabas Drug Support ran outreach clinics in the building, Friends in Need met weekly, and, most recently, Prostate Cancer Awareness has shared the accommodation. The very last group to use a room has been St John Ambulance, who moved in May 2002, six weeks before the office closed!

Alongside this liaison, development and support work, CVS has to be active in finding new volunteers. Photographs show how display boards have been used, in shop windows, supermarket foyers, in churches and at shows. Leaflets and posters have been designed and distributed, talks given, newspaper columns written. The Manchester Road office window has been used constantly as our public notice board. And money has had to be raised. County and Borough grants have throughout been the main income for CVS, but Wilmslow has always worked hard at trying to raise more – thanks to committed volunteers who have over the years held concerts and coffee mornings, dances and car boot sales, flag days and house to house collections. Records mention barbecues, bridge drives, sponsored swims, fashion shows and wine and cheese evenings – and record varying degrees of success. For many years the CVS Autumn Fair was a high spot on the calendar of those with an eye for a bargain. For most of the 1990s this would be held at the British Legion off Grove Street and earned CVS around £1,000 or more each year. And Green Shield stamps, by the way, were collected in the office from anyone who was happy to donate them, so that raffle prizes could be obtained in exchange.

Air miles and petrol coupons were also accumulated, to swap for gifts.

Volunteers have always been the manpower in all these efforts, supported by the one or two paid workers in the office. It is interesting to read that there was a pay increase for staff in 1982, when their hourly remuneration went up to £1.50! No mention of what it was before! But the minutes do record there had been no increase for two years and in 1977 pay was described as 'derisory'. By the end of the '80s rates were raised to the dizzy height of £2.50. In 1986, the Treasurer reported that the extent of cash in hand was due in part to 'scrooge like' spending control by staff and volunteers. CVS was always a make do and mend sort of a place, and no-one went to work for CVS to make their fortune! There is a note of considerable optimism behind the report to a committee meeting in January 1988, that there would be a meeting with the County Planning Resource Committee 'which would hopefully result in an increase of 40% in CVS' grant'.

It would be well into the 1990s before staff received rates of pay recommended by national pay scales. But by then, CVS in Wilmslow was no longer administering salaries and its own funds. It was recognised that Macclesfield District CVS was the registered charity and that the funding of the three offices in Macclesfield, Wilmslow and Knutsford would be managed centrally. A newly drafted constitution was discussed at length and accepted, and CVS in Wilmslow held its last AGM in the summer of 1993. Another milestone had been reached.

There is plenty more that could be written about our history, and certainly more about the many dedicated people who have played their part in our past and those who still work with us. Office and Volunteer Bureau staff, Committee members, Chairmen and Treasurers over the years, office volunteers, fundraisers, volunteers who have gone off to work in all manner of jobs across the Borough and beyond – the names would be too many to mention. So I shall leave just the two, early in this piece, of the first two Voluntary Service Organizers, who started the tradition of hard work and commitment that has been a feature of CVS in Wilmslow over the years.

Oh! And the lamb soup? A minute from March 1986 reports that 'ten tons of tinned lamb soup had been donated for CVS to dispose of'. It was clearly appreciated – the following committee meeting in July was told it had 'all gone'.

*Denise Soussi - District Volunteering Officer,*
*Macclesfield District CVS*

In the year 1772 the Lindow Workhouse Charity, now known as the Lindow Workhouse Trust, was founded on land donated by the Dowager Countess of Stamford, the Earl of Stamford, Humphrey Trafford Esq., Samuel Finney Esq., and Thomas Page Esq., with the intention of lodging, maintaining and employing the poor of the Townships of Pownall Fee, Bollin Fee, Chorley and Fulshaw in the parish of Wilmslow.

In the year 2002 this charity, established some 230 years ago, is still very much an active organization liaising with local churches, schools, surgeries and advice bureaus to determine those who are in conditions of need, and seeking to assist them financially to achieve their social and educational goals.

The following extract tells us something of the charity's origins and traditions, and is taken from notes made by Mr J.G. Harris (Clerk for the Trust) attending the Lindow Workhouse Trust Bicentenary Meeting in December 1972 – the article has been kindly donated by Group Captain Jack Buckley.

## Lindow Workhouse Trust

*On 16 October 1772 the Stamford and Trafford Estates conveyed fifteen Cheshire acres to trustees for the purpose of building a workhouse and helping the poor of the Parish of Wilmslow – this was the commencement of the Lindow Workhouse Trust. A number of the Donors' signatures were witnessed by Mr Isaac Worthington, Junior, who was one of the then partners and a predecessor of the present firm who have been your Solicitors and Clerks since the inception of the Trust.*

*The first meeting of the Trustees with Mr Samuel Finney as Chairman was held in the Wilmslow Parish Church on the 18 March 1773. At this meeting Mr Worthington was instructed to supply and keep books of record for the Trustees.*

*Further Grants of four, sixteen and eight Cheshire acres were made in 1775.*

*In the year 1837 the Poor Law Act came into force and the Old Workhouse became obsolete and was converted into two dwelling houses.*

'After leaving His Majesty's Forces in 1919 I attended as an articled Clerk my first meeting of the Trustees in June 1920. Colonel Greg was the Chairman and the meeting was held in an upstairs room of the Workhouse occupied by the farmer and his family – the meeting was followed by lunch in the kitchen – the menue [sic] was always the same roast beef carved for many years by one of the Trustees, James Wood, followed by a mixture of plum pudding and rice pudding – the youngest present (yours truly)

---

LINDOW WORKHOUSE TRUST.

————

COPIES OF GRANTS

OF PARTS OF

LINDOW COMMON,

WILMSLOW,

FOR THE USE OF THE

POOR OF WILMSLOW PARISH.

*Front cover of 'Copies of Grants of Parts of Lindow Common, Wilmslow, for the use of the poor of Wilmslow Parish'. (Courtesy Lindow Workhouse Trust)*

---

sat with his back to the fire which was of roasting proportions.

There was a celebration of 150 years in 1922 and perusing my father's notes he mentions that the then annual income was about £550 per annum – this has now risen to over £1,000 per annum. This increase over a period of fifty years may be considered modest but not when you remember that investment was restricted to chief rents or Trustee investments for most of the period.'

# 4 Chilling Tales and Enigmas

## The edge

*Prize-winner*

It is 1941. Here we have a handsome young Flight Lieutenant, eager to fight for his country, billeted in Wilmslow, flying from the Ringway and sometimes to be seen in the park in the mornings.

Two trainee Princess Christian nurses, only sixteen years old, bring out their charges in their big upholstered prams to take in the air, four babies to a pram, two at one end and two at the other.

From what I have seen of an old photograph, one of those nurses, Janet Morena Gill, is heart-stoppingly pretty. (Perhaps I should declare partiality here – she is my mother after all, but I still think it a fair assessment). That morning in Wilmslow Park, Janet Morena Gill we see has glossy brown hair, clear hazel eyes and an air of expectancy which has come from a romantic idea of life, which had been formed, so she tells me, mainly through reading Zane Grey novels with her sisters. She is sixteen years old, she has been sent

*Nurses and soldiers of the First World War. (Courtesy Alderley Edge Library)*

away from home to be trained and there is a war on – anything could happen.

What did happen to my mother has stayed with her for the rest of her life. She is now in her late seventies and still clearly remembers the dark haired young RAF officer who came to talk to her in the park. He was concerned about the babies in her charge. Were they orphans? Why were they in a home? Did anybody visit them? Were they distressed? It seemed an unusual concern for a young man and my mother thought that he was only using the topic to introduce himself to her, but as the hours passed and they talked more she realised why he had such an interest in children who had been separated from their parents.

It is curious to think that this very private and painful story was told to a complete stranger. But perhaps not so curious, sometimes it is easier to talk to someone with whom you have no connections, particularly when what you have to say may be hurtful to those who have been closest to you over the years. He told her that he had been walking the streets and avenues of nearby Alderley Edge looking for a house which he had seen in a recurring dream. He was certain that the house was in Alderley Edge because he had been amazed to recognise the streets of his dream as he had walked through the village on a hiking party trip up the Edge a few weeks ago. Now, although the streets still seemed familiar, the house remained tantalisingly hard to find. It was a large house, mostly made of brick, light in colour with ivy growing around some of the windows. In his dream the house was filled with soldiers and nurses. It was summer and the soldiers, who appeared to be convalescing, were often taken outside to sit in the sun. The period appeared to be

*Janet Morena Gill – 'Sweet sixteen and never been kissed'.*

the First World War, judging by the uniforms of the soldiers and nurses. The young Flight Lieutenant was engrossed in explaining the detail of these pictures, but it was only when my mother asked the obvious question – why was he so determined to find this house – that he told her the full extent of these recurring dreams.

He was billeted on a quiet street near Wilmslow Park and shared a pleasant house

69

with six or so other men. He was lucky in that he had his own room. It was small but comfortable, with a sagging but deliciously cosy bed and a solid wooden wardrobe and matching chest of drawers. At first he had slept well in this comfortable room, but then he had begun to have these dreams of streets and the house with its occupants from the First World War. These dreams were always laced with a sense of foreboding and he had been shocked to recognise the setting of his dreams as he walked through Alderley Edge village. Since then he had felt compelled to look for this house whenever he was given leave. Recently things had gotten much worse. He had been going to bed at the usual time only to find himself standing awake in the kitchen of the house in the early hours of the morning. Each time this happened he was sure someone had just been in the kitchen with him. But although he had looked around carefully and called softly down the corridor, he had found no-one. Two nights before he spoke to my mother, he had found himself awake in the kitchen once more as before. He had walked to the sink to pour himself a glass of water. As he waited for the tap to run cold – the antiquated plumbing was a standing joke amongst the men – he rested his arms on either side of the sink and watched the weak stream of water glinting in the reflected moonlight. He thought he heard a noise from the dark corner to the right, by the door. He turned to look and as he did so was horrified to feel a cold hand circle his left wrist and grip it firmly. Sudden pain shot through his arm and across his chest. He turned his head wildly to the left and found himself staring into dark eyes in a white face. He screamed and tried to escape, but she, for he felt sure it was a

woman, only gripped more fiercely and the pain increased as he struggled. The figure seemed to take on a more substantial form and he could hear the whispered words 'listen to me' repeated over and over. He stood still, his breath coming in great gulps, and forced himself to overcome his horror and give himself up to listen. The room around him seemed to recede and he found himself sharing some formless dark space with this apparition. He was aware of gradually being overwhelmed by some dreadful physical pain tearing at the muscles along his stomach and thighs, the pain came in great increasing waves and then he was aware of weakness creeping over him. He fell to his knees; through the hazy reality he now inhabited he could feel the cold ridges of the uneven stone floor beneath him. The physical pain receded and he was immediately filled with a dreadful mixture of loss and guilt. What had he lost? How could he live without it…without it? He sobbed as his body slumped forwards onto his arms. How could he live?

Then it was all gone. He was alone, kneeling on the kitchen floor. Above him, out of his sight, the cold water tap was still running. He would have thought that he had dreamt it but for the distinct finger marks around his wrist.

He went back to bed and slept deeply until he was awoken at the usual time by the sound of his alarm clock. Thinking of nothing but this ghostly woman, he went through the motions of an ordinary day, came home, ate, made desultory conversation with his housemates and, after a reasonable amount of time, went to bed. He lay for some time in a strange state, halfway between fear and anticipation. Would she come back? He slept.

Suddenly he was awake in the dark kitchen again. He looked around cautiously, seeking a presence. Nothing. Only the sound of his own tremulous breathing. He bent his head forward in disappointment. For a long time there was silence. Then on his left shoulder he felt a slight, almost hesitant pressure of fingers and a voice whispered again in his ear 'listen to me'. He braced himself for the pain, but none came. Instead a sense of great relaxation spread through him, a feeling which he could only describe to my mother as a tender, all encompassing, gentle love permeating his body and softly entering his mind. He sank down onto the floor and half closed his eyes. He became aware of a female figure whose form seemed to move in time with his own, and whose mouth gradually became the only focus as she spoke.

She was his mother. She had been a nurse at the house he had seen in his dreams and she had become pregnant. The house of his previous dreams now appeared around him, he was inside it. The long upper corridor – he knew where it led. He was just beginning to move along it when the images became distorted and harrowing, full of voices and fear. He could only dimly see what happened to her. He felt an echo of the physical pain he had felt on the previous night. There was a baby but it was taken away. The baby was taken away. Her feelings of loss, mixed with a guilty relief, overwhelmed him and nothing more entered his mind.

He was found the next morning by the housekeeper. Nothing much was said. She made him a cup of tea and asked him if he wanted toast. There were other men there who had shared similar restless nights, although their visions were of parachute jumps and the shattering of their bones.

After that night the Flight Lieutenant assumed that by some extraordinary chance he had returned close to his birthplace and that the proximity had allowed his past to invade his present. He told my mother that it was not possible to doubt these dreams. He knew the story they had told him was the true one of himself. He was profoundly shocked. In all of his secure comfortable life he had never been told that he had been adopted into the family of which he was now a part. Even to say the words felt strange. He had never had any intimation that anything like that could be possible. His parents were his and he was their son. He could not even bring himself to confront them with his dreams. He did not want to let the wild ghostly creature of his real mother into his life. He was sure that she was dead and that she had been dead for a long time. Perhaps she had died just after he had been born. He was certain that the images he had seen were of a past reality and not some strange fantasy of his own. But it was a reality which he wished to remain buried.

He was all the more certain of the veracity of this new information about his origins because with the dreams came memories of his childhood. Particularly of his nanny telling him how as a baby he would cry incessantly. The sound of it was heartbreaking, she said, 'you'd think he was some poor motherless child, and nothing they could do would comfort him'. Why did she say that? Did she know? Perhaps not, said my mother. It was the sort of thing that nannies said, thinking of her own experiences. He recalled that for many years he had had terrifying nightmares which he could not articulate, where he felt that someone was trying to talk to him,

71

*'Sunning Hey'. First World War chaps over from Brookdale for tea. Courtesy Alderley Edge library.*

an hour had passed she had decided that things were going well and returned, full of conspiratorial importance, and had offered to take my mother's still sleeping pram-full back as well. This gave my mother much more time with the Flight Lieutenant than would have normally been possible for a young girl in her position. She would have continued sitting there, wearing her cape and nurse's cap, listening sympathetically as she always does, her face perhaps tilted towards him and her expression serious, as the airman told her that he could not talk to anyone in his family without causing extreme pain.

She only saw the young man once more. He met her in the park on another sunny morning when she was wheeling babies out and told her that his dreams had gone and that if one believed in spirits then this one was at rest – or at least had no more to tell him. He was to be posted away the next day and was glad he had found her there. He stood for a moment in the sunlight and then bent down, and for the sheer joy of it, kissed her. By the time she had realigned her cap and recovered her composure, he had gone.

Janet thought about the nurse from the First World War a lot. Janet was a young woman too. She wore a nurse's uniform. When she bathed babies in her charge she thought about the mothers, their stories, but she never spoke to anyone of the young nurse in 1916 and her child. Until she told me. Of course, I asked her for more concrete evidence. The young man's name? Did she ever find out the name of the street – the house – the people concerned? She could not clearly remember. In the weeks after he had talked to her she had visited Alderley Edge out of curiosity. She asked about convalescent homes used for soldiers

someone who would not leave him alone. Could this have been her – his mother – trying to tell him about his birth and her love? He was quiet after saying this, remembering the feeling of deep love which he had experienced. It was good to have felt that. It would be good to have it to think of in the future.

And so eventually he finished telling this story to my mother, sitting on a bench in the park in Wilmslow in 1941. The other trainee nurse had taken her charges back to the home, not wishing to disturb what had seemed to be a budding romance, and after in the First World War; there had been names given – she remembered a name with 'Oak' in it and another with 'Hay' or perhaps 'Hey', but what was most important in her memory was the distress of this young man and the certainty with which she accepted his story.

I really didn't give it much credence – thinking it sounded like a romantic tale told by a young man who wanted to impress a pretty girl – until recently, in Alderley Edge library, where I came across some photographs of soldiers and nurses standing outside a house of brick covered with Ivy. On the back of the photograph are the words 'Sunning Hey. First World War – Chaps from Brookdale' – and I felt that there is something more someone wants me to know.

*F.M.M. Macleod*

## Killed by a bell

If you go into St Bartholomew's church and turn left to reach the west end under the tower you will find a small doorway. This gives access to the spiral staircase leading to the bells at the top of the tower. Above the doorway is a stone tablet with the following inscription: John, son of Robert and Penelope Hunt, was killed by the first bell on Sunday 30 August 1767.

How was he killed? What was he doing among the bells on that fateful Sunday? Who discovered him? Was he alone when it happened? How could someone be killed by a bell anyway?

Unfortunately we have very little further information. The burial registers reveal that John was thirteen at the time of his death, but other details of the accident have not

*The stone tablet accounting for the young John Hunt's death, Wilmslow Parish church.*

*The bell that killed John Hunt.*

survived. To understand what may have happened, and maybe devise your own explanation, it is necessary to know something about the bell itself and how it is rung.

The bell which killed John Hunt is the treble bell of the peal of six bells, cast at Gloucester by Abraham Rudhall in 1733, and still in regular use to this day. It is shown in the photograph, mouth upwards and ready for ringing. It weighs 5 cwt (1/4 ton) and is 30 inches in diameter. When rung by means of the rope attached to the wheel, it takes about two seconds to swing round in a full circle until it is again mouth upwards, it then sounds once before swinging round the other way and sounding again.

Imagine then that you are John Hunt. Possibly you find that the door to the stairway is not locked and curiosity leads you to venture upwards. There is another door giving access to the gloomy bell chamber with six silent bells all mouth upwards, ready for ringing. You enter and stand near to the smallest of the six looking around in wonderment at the scene before you and quite ignorant of the mechanics of the bells. As you watch the bell starts to move and, to your horror, you realise there is no time and no space to escape. You have learned very quickly, and too late, how bells work, and that 5 cwt of bell-shaped bronze with the inscription 'peace and good neighbourhood' can be deadly.

This is pure speculation of course. Perhaps you have a more plausible explanation. Perhaps some day a document will be discovered telling us what really did happen to poor John Hunt, aged thirteen.

*Derek Smith*

# The enigma of the chapel in the woods

In the early part of the last century, a chapel existed in the Carr's Wood, and could certainly be found intact surrounded by an iron railing in the late 1920's and early 1930's.

There is no mention of the chapel on the 1872 Ordnance Survey map, but the six-inch Ordnance Survey map for 1911 shows a disused chapel towards the end of the woods near to the present Carrwood Road. My recollections are that the chapel was not so far along the woods, but time has a habit of distorting the memory.

The chapel fell into disrepair, and by the late 1950's all that remained were the foundations and a number of large stones strewn around the woods in the vicinity of the chapel site.

Rumours abounded in the early part of the century that the chapel was linked by underground passages to one of the local halls and to the Parish church. The latter is highly unlikely due to the distance involved and the terrain. The former is possible since the nearest hall would have been Pownall Hall, and that would have been about 300 metres (250 yards) as the crow flies, that is if the disused chapel on the 1911 map was the one in question. The chapel and Pownall Hall would also be roughly on the same height above sea level, which would not be true of the church and the chapel.

I can offer no information as to the denomination of the chapel or to the details of the interior, as the chapel was no longer extant when I first saw the site, the building did appear to have been added to and renovated over a period of time. Many of the stones from which the chapel was built were decorated in an early Christian style, and one stone in particular clearly displayed the first and last letters of the Greek alphabet intertwined, which have Christian significance. It is these stones and others bearing inscriptions, which were strewn about the site well into the sixties, which are to me an enigma.

The inscribed stones were of various types and on some the lettering was illegible. Whether they were from an original chapel on the site or were brought there from elsewhere remains a mystery.

There are two stones of particular interest. The first indicates that the chapel was dedicated to St Olaf. This refers to Olaf Tryggvason, King of Norway from AD 995 to AD 1000, who was converted to Christianity in England in AD 994. and then returned to Norway in AD 995 to depose the pagan Earl Hakon. He helped to bring Christianity to Iceland, Greenland, the Faeroes and large parts of Norway, until he was succeeded by King Canute.

The second stone of interest may very well reinforce this connection between King Olaf I, and Hakon, since the inscription appears to read: 'The ring of Hacon the apostate which Olaf securely hung behind the temple door'. Was Hacon the Norse Earl the Hacon mentioned above? Clearly it is a Norse or Viking name, as indeed Olaf was, but at least we know that Hacon was a converted pagan. This is indicated by the use of the word 'apostate', which means one who has renounced or changed his faith. This word did not come into use in the English language until the fourteenth century.

To summarise then, we have a chapel built in the Carr's Wood consisting in part of stones decorated and inscribed in an early Christian style. The stones recall events of the Viking period, as well they may since there were early Christian Viking communities in the Wirral and Chester areas, and Knutsford only six miles away

*The stone depicting the Ring of Hacon.*

was listed in the Domesday book as Cunetesford, an obvious link with King Canute the successor of King Olaf, or as he became known, St Olaf. The style of the inscriptions on the stones however is not of that period. If the stones had been inscribed prior to the fifteenth century they would most certainly have been in Latin. The shape of the letters, the style of the inscriptions and the use of words like 'apostate' would indicate that the inscriptions were probably produced in the late nineteenth century in a style intended to mimic that of the Celtic period. The Victorians were obsessed with the Middle Ages and the Celtic Legends and they produced a lot of artefacts in a pseudo-Celtic style. A prominent example of this obsession is *The Idylls of the King* written by Alfred Lord Tennyson in the 1870's and based on *Morte d'Arthur* written around 1485 by Sir Thomas Malory.

I doubt if the inscribed stones in the Carr's Wood are those of an earlier chapel, and I suspect that the Victorians created them around 1880 in this pseudo-Celtic style. They relate to the stories surrounding St Olaf, since the chapel was dedicated to that Norse saint. I could of course be wrong and there may have been a much earlier chapel on the same site, hence the rumours of the underground passage, it is of course possible that the Victorians added the inscribed stones to other stones which already existed. If so, are we to assume that the stones were imported into the

*The chapel in the Carr's Wood.*

Wilmslow area purely for the building of the chapel, or is there a deeper reason? Could it be that Wilmslow, or as it was known in earlier times – Le Bolyn – is the site of an earlier Christian chapel? Perhaps we will never know the answers to these questions. It is over forty years since I saw the stones and their inscriptions, and I suspect that they have long vanished and the inscriptions have been weathered into illegibility, but the stones in the Carr's Wood will always remain an intrigue.

*Dr K.A. Hollin*

# 5  War Memories

## 'A pleasant place to live'
*Prize-winner*

In 1939, when I first came to live in Wilmslow with my parents, it was a village. Admittedly the largest village in England, but nonetheless a village with a pleasant atmosphere, a community spirit, friendly Cheshire people and fields all round. Indeed isn't the motto of Wilmslow 'A Pleasant Place to Live'?

Bruce Butcher (who will be a familiar name to many of the older residents) and I got engaged the day war broke out. We only had a few days together before he left to join his ship. As a Cunard Ship's Officer (we met on board the Queen Mary) he was immediately transferred to the Royal Navy, on 20 August 1939. His first appointment was Contraband Control in the English Channel. Subsequently he spent twenty months in charge of a minesweeper in Lagos Harbour, Nigeria. So I was left to wait for two years before we were married. I wanted to be here when he got home, so when I was called up I opted to join the Women's Land Army. It would have been nice to be a Wren but then I could have been sent

*Mrs Joan Butcher – then Miss Loan Chasney – out riding at Pownall Hall Farm.*

*Bank Square, Wilmslow, 1911. (Courtesy Cheshire Libraries and Museums)*

anywhere and I wanted to be here when Bruce came back.

The job of milkmaid at Pownall Hall Farm, which was a farm then, was allotted to me. This entailed going for the milk churns to another farm on Altrincham Road, going back to the dairy, cooling and bottling the milk; driving round Pownall Park and Macclesfield Road to deliver the milk, getting back to the farm for a hot cocoa to book in how much and what the customers had received; going back to the dairy to wash all the bottles and sterilise everything with a hot steam nozzle. I started at 7 a.m. and finished at 2 p.m, seven days a week, and earned sixteen shillings (80p).

Wilmslow was quite different in those days. Grove Street was full of cars going both ways. The only shop that still remains (I think) is Charnley's the Chemists; there was a Saddlers with saddles in the window and reins hanging from nails on the walls – nice smell of leather in there – and a shop that sold animal feed, corn, bird seed and various other old-fashioned things. There was a Woolworth's, which went right through to Green Lanes, with a door opposite the police station. This was quite

*Bruce Butcher (Joan's husband) leading the RAF ladies down Church Street on Civic Survey.*

unusual but not needed as the little arcade was always there. There was a café called The Harlequin, with a little paved garden in front of it. Bank Square had four banks open for business four hours a day. On the corner of Hawthorn Lane was a department store called Clegg's which sold clothes, materials by the yard, baby linen, haberdashery and bed linen, and had a small restaurant in the basement. There were three butchers, a fish shop (Mac Fisheries), two or three grocers, two bakers, a fruit and vegetable shop and a plumber with a window display which had for it's

centrepiece a white WC! There were hardly any shops in Hawthorn Lane or Water Lane. There were a few shops beside the Rex and a few on the other side of Alderley Road that stopped at Dr Finney's house, which was where Lloyds Bank is now. On Green Lane there was a smithy that shod horses, and behind that was an auction room and a garage that went through to Grove Street.

The Rex and the British Legion Hall on the old Market Place (now Safeways) were the social centers. Every Saturday night the Rex changed its programme, so seats were booked and you met all your friends, the programme was: the news, followed by a small feature film and then the movie – no adverts! We had radios in our houses but no television (or computers, or the Internet). We did have pianos and usually someone in the family could play – in my house it was my mother.

The Legion Hall during the war was the meeting place for all sorts of things, plays put on by the Green Room, charity fundraising, civic receptions, dances, concerts, lectures, and there was the Drill Hall for the Home Guard. But, as the war progressed, and the RAF camp site (on which I now live in Summerfields) became enormous, the Legion Hall became a venue

for entertaining the troops, along with a Church Army hut on the bit of ground by the church, which is now the Garden of Remembrance. I worked at both these places as a WVS bod. The RAF camp was huge – apparently every ranker in the RAF passed through Wilmslow at some time, and there were plenty of WAAF's too. I had some strange, delightful, and horrible experiences (inevitably) whilst I worked there, but mostly they were splendid lads and easy to manage, unless they had had a few too many beers in the local pubs. On one memorable occasion, two of us WVS' were working in the Church Army hut and there were only two or three 'customers'.

*Bruce Butcher, then Chairman of Wilmslow Council, greeting the Duke of Edinburgh at the opening of Manchester Airport.*

Above: *Bruce and Joan Butcher with their son John. (Courtesy Joan Butcher)*

*Bruce Butcher at the opening of Styal Women's Priso. (Courtesy Joan Butcher)*

My companion left early to have her hair washed as her husband was due home that night. After a little while the doors opened wide and in came a stream of Air Force Blue uniforms, hundreds! So I said: 'If you want anything to eat, boys, you'll have to help me'. They were great. One made toast, one tea, one heated baked beans, one scrambled eggs, and in no time they were all fed and watered – and they washed up and left everything ship-shape afterwards!

We were never hungry, but food was so boring – grey bread, puddings and cakes made with dried eggs. We had plenty of vegetables and fruit in season, but we didn't see bananas or peaches. Personally, we were lucky, as we had friends in the US, Canada and Australia, who sent us food parcels which made a big difference, and if you knew a farmer you could sometimes manage to get a chicken and some fresh eggs.

Sometimes we had parades for various reasons, for instance for Wings for Victory. While I was in the Land Army we had a contingent (four of us!) in these parades – one time I was late to join up at the Rex car park and the parade was starting to go down Water Lane. Driving the car with my mother and a friend aboard, I passed the parade and a policeman in the middle of the road had to jump smartly out of the way - I was had up for dangerous driving and fined ten shillings! The policeman was very nice about it when I apologised to him, but in truth I hadn't even seen him, thank God I didn't hit him!

We were very sheltered in Wilmslow; we did have a few bombs dropped on us in 1940, and four more in 1943. One house in Broadway was demolished in the first attack, and half a house in Macclesfield Road in the second attack. We could see the red glow in the sky the night Manchester burned.

As the war progressed and all of Europe fell to the Nazi onslaught, it became very worrying. I remember walking along Parkway wondering how I would cope if we were invaded, being young and female it was a daunting prospect. At our lowest ebb the speeches that Churchill made really pulled us all through. And then we heard of the wonderful courage of the few. A cousin of mine living in Kent has told me how they watched the dogfights in the air overhead, and marvelled at the brilliance of the fighter pilots in their Spitfires. A friend of mine who was one of 'the few' had said to me some years before the war had started: 'If war comes, it will be individual combat in the air, and the best pilots will win and survive'. He was right, and he did survive. We didn't know it then, but I suppose as Churchill said, this was our finest hour.

I was one of the lucky wives, as my husband survived despite a very dangerous war. Bruce was aboard the aircraft carrier, HMS *Eagle* for six months. The ship was finally sunk on 10 August 1942, during the Pedestal Convoy an event that literally saved Malta from the enemy. Bruce swam in the Mediterranean for two hours until a destroyer picked him up. A young Sub-Lieutenant hauled him up the climbing ropes onto the deck of the destroyer. We met this man again, ten years later, at a dance in Newcastle. They recognised each other!

After 'survivors leave', Bruce was sent to Skye where HMS *Agamemnon* and two other large ships were making sorties to the far North Sea and laying hundreds of mines – very nerve racking. He got compassionate leave to come back home a few days after our first child was born. He

*Joan and Bruce Butcher (centre) celebrating Rose Queen Day at Lindow End.*

then did a spell in North America, followed by a further year in the Pacific and the Far East, as the Japanese had to be defeated too. His last job with the navy was in charge of the Manchester canal, where the Navy had presence, so we were here for VE Day and we all went, little John as well, to see the bonfire lit in the Carrs. We all sang songs and were so happy - but if my memory serves me well, no fireworks were allowed.

Wilmslow has been home to me for all these years (sixty-three in all, with a few breaks). My daughter was born here too, then confirmed and married in St Bartholomew's; my parents died here, as did my husband three years ago. My memories of this place are happy and sad, they are of wonderful friends, kind, helpful people, marvellous scenery only minutes away; the music, theatre and culture of Manchester on our doorstep, to say nothing of the Commonwealth Games. We have seen enormous growth – inevitable with our geographic position, so near to the airport, main line trains and motorways, but Wilmslow is still 'A Pleasant Place to Live', and my place.

*Joan Butcher*

*Joan Butcher celebrating a recent birthday.*

## 'Make do and mend' (wartime memories)

Shortly before the outbreak of war in 1939 various preparations were underway, including the building of air-raid shelters. We had lived in Wilmslow since 1929, but now life was about to change. Although our father was ill at the time – he died in 1940 – he had a capacious shelter dug in the back garden. Sadly the subsoil was clay and so it rapidly filled with water. Fortunately our house had a coal cellar with a convenient exit into the garden via the coal chute; this was protected by a wall low enough to climb over and about a foot wide. The top was planted with colourful flowers and bulbs. My brother, sister and I – all teenagers – built a somewhat lopsided baffle wall in bricks and mortar to protect the inner door of the coal cellar where we slept on spartan metal bunks during the thankfully infrequent raids. During one raid a land mine was dropped behind the Rex cinema – from our cellar it sounded as if someone was wheeling a barrow load of bricks over our heads, dropping them as they went.

Because of our father's army experiences in France during the First World War, when invading armies had rampaged down the main highways, he wanted to give us as much protection as he could, in case Alderley Road were to suffer a similar fate. So, to complete our defences, a high baffle wall was built outside the bay window of the dining room, giving us, if necessary, one room above ground practically free from the possibility of flying glass or other missiles, and thus condemning the room to almost perpetual twilight. This didn't really matter, however, as fire regulations decreed that attics had to be cleared of their contents because of the risk of incendiary bombs, so an odd assortment of lumber ended up being moved down and stored in the dining room.

Another aspect of father's forward thinking was that he foresaw the shortages to come, so he gave us money to buy clothes. We went to Edith Dennett's dress shop in Grove Street and I bought a bottle-green woollen dress, a rather nice fitted, pale blue coat and ten pairs of silk stockings. Only the coat survived the war.

This was the period of evacuees, and one day – 3 September 1939 – I sat in a deckchair on the pavement outside our house with a friend and waited for children that had been evacuated from Liverpool to be delivered. They came by car and it was my job to then drive an allotted child to his or her new 'family'. While I was sitting there a passer-by told me that they had just heard on the wireless that war had been declared.

More evacuees arrived. My mother was the billeting officer dealing with mothers and infants, and at the end of one hectic day she found herself taking home two mothers and three infants instead of the one family she had been expecting. It was a good job our spare room had twin beds! When the air raids lessened they returned to Liverpool and were replaced in our house by Fred, a charming schoolboy from a more vulnerable part of Liverpool. After the war, and having moved to another part of Wilmslow, we were amazed and delighted one day when the tall, handsome young man who roared up to our front door on a motorcycle, turned out to be Fred.

Then there was Gladys, a corporal in the ATS, who worked at the tank depot at Handforth. Our final 'evacuee' after all the others had departed was our widowed aunt who lived with us till she re-married at the end of the war. Her responsibility in the running of the household was the shopping. She attired herself with shopping bags, ration books, and the all-important shooting stick with rubber ferrule to rest her legs while queuing, then she sallied forth – a real hunter-gatherer – to battle. The constant fluctuation in numbers in the household didn't make her task any easier; our house had become a centre for rest and recuperation for the various members of families on leave or holiday from the forces, the medical and nursing professions, and the colleges. One of our visitors was a cousin from South Africa who had been a prisoner of war and who, on repatriation, spent a short time with us on his way back home. Following the meagre rations at the POW

*Alderley Road, Wilmslow. (Courtesy The Valentines Series)*

*Mrs Groves' mother, Mrs Sharratt – the ambulance driver.*

camp he insisted that all meals should be divided up into strictly equal portions, and he also ate every scrap - even fish skin which he said contained phosphorous – we were very glad he didn't insist on equality in that instance.

In the early days of the war our mother joined the Civil Defence and drove an ambulance, for which she had to take a test whilst wearing a gas mask. This proved a rather tricky exercise as she wore spectacles. As they gradually steamed up she sent a silent prayer hoping that the policeman testing her would pass her before she was completely unable to see. Much to her relief he did. We managed to dissuade her from volunteering to drive a bus from Wilmslow Station to Moor Lane – even though she had driven a grocers van in London for a short time during the First World War – we thought a bus was a bit too much.

At the beginning of the war mother's car was put into hibernation – supported on bricks with the wheels and rotor arm removed, thus making it of no use to an invading enemy. It was later resurrected as a Sitting Cases car and mother was given a smart uniform to wear whilst she ferried patients to and from hospital clinics.

Our brother was a member of the Home Guard before he was called up, he was probably more efficient than Private Pyke, and he had a real rifle. Wielding the rifle, he held up and questioned drivers on Alderley Road, near the Wizard (a very well-sited guard post), in the early hours of the morning.

In the camaraderie and trusting spirit of the time, lifts were freely given and hospitality often offered. When our brother was in Holland shortly after D-Day, our mother saw a solitary Dutch sailor, picked him up and brought him home for tea, secretly hoping that her son would meet with some mother in Holland who would do the same for him. After that the sailor came to visit a few times before being posted on elsewhere.

Everybody tackled some form of voluntary war work, encouraged by such slogans as 'Make do and Mend' and 'Dig for Victory'. Some made camouflage netting for aircraft and gun emplacements, others volunteered to serve lunches in the British Restaurant where you could have a two-course lunch for a shilling (but only if you had a voucher), and others mended the woollen socks of the Morley gunners who guarded the parachute training centre at Ringway Airfield – the army laundry had shrunk the socks, but not the holes, to half size. I remember making a housecoat out of furnishing brocade and having a jacket and skirt made out of one of my father's suits. We dug up the back lawn and in the virgin soil we grew vegetables, there were cabbages and sprouts and enormous cauliflowers which we took to the Alderley Cottage Hospital. One of our catchphrases from the war was the redoubtable Mrs Clegg's exhortation to our mother whilst she helped spread meagre rations of butter onto sandwiches for the airmen of the RAF camp – 'Scrape it on and scrape it off Mrs Sharratt!'

But life was not all work – there were the tea dances at the Rex cinema attended by officers stationed nearby, which enlivened Saturday afternoons. And knitting was an occupation that could be enjoyed and carried out almost anywhere. As the type of garments knitted – scarves, balaclava helmets and shapeless pullovers – meant that no great concentration was needed and poor light no hindrance, we knitted all over – whilst reading – at the cinema – and

*Mrs Grove's mother and brother – ambulance driver and Home Guard.*

*The Rex Buildings, Wilmslow. (Courtesy The Valentines Series)*

*Bank Square Gardens, Wilmslow. (Courtesy The Valentines Series)*

when our father was having heat treatment at the Alderley Cottage Hospital the physio didn't waste any of her time, she knitted. Time wasn't wasted either when travelling by bus, the space between the overhead grab-rail and the luggage rack afforded a convenient gap through which to push a ball of wool so that it didn't roll about on the floor whilst you knitted your way to Manchester!

Wilmslow was the police centre for air raid incidents, and during college holidays a friend and I would spend evenings manning phone lines for outlying police stations reporting in. The small room where we worked was crammed with wooden pillars supporting the ceiling, reinforced by a network of more beams on the floor which tripped you up whenever you moved. There were two officers on duty – a fatherly, silver-haired one, and a younger constable who spoke only about his ongoing rows with his wife, which culminated in him throwing a teapot at her. I was relieved to find that policemen were human, if not always to be relied on domestically.

One evening as my friend Janetta and I walked home from the station in the dark, we heard a snoring noise coming from the back of the New Inn. We told our policemen the next evening and the fatherly one walked back with us thinking it might be a tramp. We were disappointed when he wouldn't let us stay while he investigated, but after all the excitement it turned out only to be roosting barn owls.

Shortly after this incident I left Wilmslow to go and nurse in London. I married and have since lived away from Wilmslow, but I remember it as a pleasant place in which to grow up.

*Mrs B. Grove*

# War in Wilmslow

I was born at 'Fernleigh', Altrincham Road, Wilmslow, in October 1931. During the '30s we moved to 'Albury', 20 Hawthorn Lane, Wilmslow, where I lived with my father, Harold, my mother, Doris (Dot), and my elder brother. We spent the war years in Hawthorn Lane and I well remember listening to the radio when Neville Chamberlain told us we were 'at war with Germany'.

We at once began converting our cellar into an air-raid shelter, this did not take long, and we gave up after a while as we needed an escape exit which meant some work outside. Father then took us to the Umbro factory where workers were busy digging air-raid shelters in a garden behind the cottages in Water Lane in the spare ground near the works. I will always remember at that time a Fairey Battle Plane flew over quite low and that gave us all heart and confidence of victory. Of course the 'Battle' was no match for the Germans and they were quickly withdrawn.

The next chore was being fitted with gas masks, the smell of which was terrible, and this was followed with the issue of identity cards, my number was LFXM-11-4.

After the air-raid shelter in the cellar was completed we felt reassured that we would be safe and secure from Hitler's bombs. The time arrived for the first warning which came in the form of a policeman on his bike blowing his whistle and shouting 'air-raid take cover'. Of course it was a false alarm so we all trooped back to bed.

The next time was more memorable. We were alerted by the wail of the siren that had been installed at the police station, so off we all went down to the cellar while father went off to the AFS point. Mother, John and I were making ourselves comfortable when a large toad crawled out from somewhere - we immediately collected our belongings and evacuated back upstairs! We never used the shelter again, and as it happened the whole thing had been a false alarm.

About this time we were shown round the Ack Ack battery on Oversley Ford, I presume it was there to protect Ringway Airport, a fat lot of use it would have been, although it did fire a salvo on one day when I was sat on the toilet reading the *Dandy*. The guns started to fire without warning, and what a shock it was, but it was good to see where the four shells had burst and made a perfect square in the sky. I didn't see any planes that day, so I don't know what they could have been firing at.

Our spirits were soon lifted again when an ME109, brought down by an RAF sixty-footer, was put on display in the Rex car park.

The RAF camp on Eight Acres was now complete, and recruits came from all over the UK. Suddenly there was a need for entertainment in Wilmslow as the men could find little to do when they were allowed out. It was noted that the Church Army had a canteen on what is now the Memorial Garden, and it was the staff at Umbro who felt that they could organize a similar thing for the RAF men. A Forces canteen was duly opened above Jaffrey's Plumbers in Green Lane, but soon became so popular that it was moved to the larger Umbro Works canteen. Crockery supplies for the canteen were made up from donations by the people from round and about, most gave anything they could, but of course we did come up against the odd old grump! An immense amount of credit must go to the Umbro staff who gave their time freely and without complaint to ensure the success of the canteen, and so helped the welfare of the Forces.

It was decided that besides 'digging for victory' we had enough room in at No. 20 to keep some hens. These were purchased from Mr Massey on the peat bog, whom incidentally, taught John and I how to cut peat to supplement our coal ration at home.

After a while we had plenty of eggs and now and again we had enough rations to feed more than ourselves, so John and I were sent to the village to invite a couple of servicemen back for lunch. We did this whenever possible and increased our popularity with the men by letting them haves baths in the comfort of our home.

We had two soldiers, Dave and Ron, who billeted with us for a time before they were sent to the Middle East. We knew that was where they had gone because we got a letter from them, but after that never received any further news. We also had two girl evacuees with us for a time during the Blitz.

There was great excitement one day when a barrage balloon which 'sailed' over the Carrs got chased by some air force personnel; they were worried that the loose cabling might cause some damage or injury. I don't know what happened to it after it flew off towards Manchester!

The well-known pianists Ranvicz and Landauer had a house in Pownall Park, as far as I remember it was the third on the left after the gates. They had two pianos in the front room and it was great to listen to them practising.

The RAF dance band was stationed at the camp for a while and gave a concert at the Rex. I was lucky enough to attend. As for indoors, our main amusement was of course the radio. We were allowed to listen to Churchill's speeches, and to some of the programmes such as ITMA, *Into Battle*, and the news.

Mr Churchill formed an Air Parachute Regiment and the training was undertaken at the Ringway, with Whitely aircraft transporting the men to Tatton Park to practice their parachuting. Alas, one of the Whitely's crashed on 'The Circuit' off Moor Lane killing some people. (Incidentally, years after the war my father sat next to a blind man at Manchester Airport, the man asked my father to describe the airport to him as he had trained in the parachute regiment before going into action where he was blinded.)

We, of course, were always collecting something to aid the war effort; paper, aluminium; anything to help.

In 1940-41 we had the Manchester Blitz, and following the toad affair in our air-raid shelter, we had decided not to return. We had a window which looked towards Manchester; mother arranged chairs so that when the siren warnings came we could gather on the chairs and watch the dreadful 'fireworks'.

One night a plane that was obviously in trouble jettisoned its bomb at too low an altitude. It took off a chimney pot in Grove Avenue, carried on over the Conservative Club and Mrs Meads school, over Water Lane and into the side of one of the cottages. As far as I remember the name of the inhabitants were a Mr and Mrs Bradbury, who were sitting in their downstairs room by the fire when the bomb came through, luckily they weren't severely hurt. It was fortunate that the bomb didn't explode as it was a 1000 kgm bomb, one of the largest dropped in the North West at that time – it would certainly have made a mess of Wilmslow. The bomb disposal squad were of course notified, but they were so busy that they could not diffuse the

*The Carrs, Wilmslow. (Courtesy The Valentines Series)*

bomb for about seven days, meaning that everyone for a fair distance had to be evacuated. The Umbro factory and Wycliffe Avenue school closed, and most of Water Lane, Kennerleys Lane and Grove Avenue were also cordoned off. The officer who diffused the bomb was French and I was told by one of his squad that he sat astride the bomb and took the fuse out with a hammer and chisel – I assume that they had removed the explosive before trying this! I always remember that the fins of the bomb were bright blue and I still have a piece of the bomb that was given to my father by the Frenchman. The bomb was taken away in a lorry with soldiers sitting astride it.

Ringway Airport was a collecting point for American aircraft which were supplied via the Lend Lease Pact. There were many Hudson aircraft there, but then they stopped us going to see them and the road was closed.

Bill Thorn, one of the best test pilots at A.V. Roe, Woodford, lived in Hall Road and he was a very nice gentleman - walked straight as a ramrod, and when he asked my father if he would like to fly in a Lancaster the offer was not refused. When the big day came mother, John and I stood in the back garden with a large white tablecloth to wave. Sure enough this Lancaster came over flying very low and we waved the cloth and father saw us. While up there he asked Bill Thorn over the intercom, 'how many times has this plane flown?' 'Oh', replied Bill, 'this is the first time it's been off the ground'. Unfortunately Bill was killed in the Tudor crash behind Woodford church after the war had ended.

Great excitement! American troops had arrived! They were stationed in the large house on the corner of Kennerleys Lane and Hawthorn Lane amongst others in the area.

Of course they were very welcome and our house became a 'bath house' for the troops who were very appreciative. They gave us much food, gum ('any gum chum?'), but most of all I recall the aroma of the instant coffee they had in their 'K' rations. Instant coffee was developed by Nescafe especially for the soldiers, so I suppose we were amongst the first people in the UK to taste instant coffee.

My pal, David Garner, and I were asked by the GI's if we knew of a field where they could play baseball. David, always one with the eye for the main chance, said he knew of several, and would show them provided he and I could show them the way in one of their armoured cars. As it turned out it wasn't quite an armoured car, but it did for the exercise – we went to Alderley, Mobberley, David had them going all ways, but we knew where we were going to end up, at 'Clarks College', now Pownall Hall School. The American GI's played against a Canadian Air Force team, it was great fun. David and I sat on the ground between the two teams whilst a newsreel was shot. Sometime later one of the GI's found out his mother had seen him on the footage in an American cinema, so David and I must have been there too!

Amusement in those days was very much self-made. Mother and her friends held 'Beetle Drives', and helped in the canteen. Grandma made the 'paste' for the canteen sandwiches – it was amazing how far she could make a tin of salmon go. We would go to see the tanks which were brought in for repair at the CWS factory in Handforth – the testing ground was where the A34 is now built. There were of course the Saturday Matinees at the Rex and Palace cinemas. We watched *Gone with the Wind* at the Palace, with tea served at the interval

Other things I remember were the Italian prisoners of war in their dark brown battle dress uniforms with a large yellow circular patch on their backs. They were put to work on the land helping the farmers.

I also loved to go into Grove Street which of course was a two way street then. The old shops – John Williams, Cleggs, Mac Fisheries, The Tureet, FC Berry's, Madame Owen, Edith Derwent, Woolworths, Plants' sweet shop, Brooks the barbers (how I loved the spray when the 'cut' was finished). Then there was The Maypole, Chadwick's (they sold the best sausages, during the war you queued for ages to get a few, a full pound if you were lucky), Watson's café shop, Locket Lloyd and Statham Electrics. Other shops were Gibbons fish and chips opposite Percival off-licence and grocery store in Water Lane – Gibbons was next to Bracegirdle's bicycle shop and garage, behind which was a wet fish shop. Jim's Fish and Chips was next to the 'Ring a Bells' pub and opposite the market place on Church Street where the British Legion Hall was, dances were held to the music of the Georgians. Then of course there was Blackshaw's fish and chip shop opposite the

'George and Dragon' in Church Street, the best fish and chips in town. Other shops that come to mind include Mossop & Hunt, Johnson's radio shop who used to supply Wilmslow with gramophone records, Sant's the newsagents, Garner's outfitters, both on Church Street, Charnley's the Chemist and the Midland Bank on Bank Square, the Williams & Deacon Bank, Jackson's Stores and Taylor the butchers in Hawthorn Street, Cyril Co-Op butchers on Grove Street, Hosgood's greengrocers, Johnstone's bookshop, and Flitcroft's.

I remember on one occasion before war broke out, my mother sent me to John Williams' for a bag of sugar which was weighed out into a big blue bag. I was given a shilling – a lot of money in those days – I got home okay, but dropped the lot on the floor once back in the kitchen, I was suitably chastised and sent for another one. This incident haunted me throughout the war when our sugar ration was measured into a jam jar each week and if you used before the week was through - well, that was it. I often thought of that sugar going in the bin because I had dropped it.

*Stuart S. Humphreys*

# 6 Buildings

## Wilmslow Parish church, St Bartholomew's

Since retiring in 1995 I have enjoyed helping in our Parish church, as assistant verger, Sexton and handyman, and as a result, meeting and talking to the many visitors who come and admire the church. In order to satisfy their questions I have researched the various records, read the history books, attended talks and now have the following answers to questions such as, 'How old is the church?', 'When was it built?', 'Who were the people who built it?'. For myself, as a result of this research, I have developed an admiration for and an acknowledgment of the religious commitment of the people who created this church over the past eight centuries.

Wilmslow Parish church has been a place of Christian worship for more than 750 years. During the past eight centuries many people have contributed in building, rebuilding, modifying and maintaining this church as a centre of worship in the Parish of Wilmslow. The following is a review of some of these contributions.

*Thirteenth century*
The Fittons' were an important family and records suggest that they started this church. The first rector was Roger Phyton (Fyton, Fitton) (1250-1300). In around 1280 Edmund Fitton dedicated a piece of land for the service of 'God and the Blessed Mary of Wilmslow'. Some of the stonework in the crypt is believed to be from this period.

*Fifteenth century*
The oldest memorial brass (dated 1460) in Cheshire is in the Prescott chapel and depicts Sir Robert del Bouthe and his wife Douce. Douce (née Venables) was a descendent of the Fitton's and was married in 1409, aged nine, and her dowry was the northern half of her family manor, which stretched from the Bollin to beyond Styal.

It is probable the base of the tower and other parts of the west end of the church date from this century.

*Sixteenth century*
The building that we see today was mainly built in Tudor times, most of it supervised by the then Rector, Henry Trafford (1515-37). He installed the fine roof; some of the bosses bear his initials and were gilded in 1979. One boss is a caricature of a Green Man with a red tongue and green leaves. It is at this time that the three chantry chapels are built/rebuilt. The Trafford (now Jesus) chapel by the Trafford family, the Booth (now Prescott) chapel for the Booth family and the Ryle chapel by Henry Ryle.

Let us pause to reflect on the importance of religion in these times. This large building was the centre of worship for the Parish

*Wilmslow Parish church.*

*Wilmslow Parish church, St Bartholomews, in the twenty-first century.*

*The Green Man, St Bartholomews.*

which then included Alderley Edge (Chorley) and Lindow, with a population of 202 householders, 1,100 people (1587). The Bishop's visitation of 1548 lists six priests.

John Dale was curate from 1584-1626 and transcribed into a book the parish records of births and burials, and thus began good quality records. Queen Elizabeth I required a locked Parish chest for the storage of these records and the Wilmslow chest can be seen in the Prescott chapel. John Dale probably carved the gravestone for his children, Phyllis (d. 1596) and Thomas. This is the oldest gravestone in the churchyard and can be seen just to the east of the Porch.

### Seventeenth century
Perhaps this century is best remembered for some negative activities. From the Parish Records it can be seen that during the Commonwealth the dissenting Minister, John Brereton, sold off the lead from the organ and font, supposedly to be used as musket balls, and replaced the font with a pewter basin and ironwork stand.

A Fitton of Fulshaw Hall installed the first pew in the middle of this century.

### Eighteenth century
John Leigh of Hawthorn Hall bought the Ryles chapel in 1700 and rebuilt it as the Hawthorn chapel. He is buried under the floor and a photograph of his lead coffin is on display in the church. Some remnants of early stained glass can be seen in this chapel – The Griffin from the Trafford coat of arms, wheat sheaves from the Fitton coat of arms, also fragments from Henry Ryle's and John Leigh's coats of arms.

### Nineteenth century
By the beginning of the Victorian period the church was in a poor state of repair.

In 1835 a box was bought for the Priest to stand on so he could keep his feet dry. The existing nave floor was so rotten that a careless footstep could have broken through on to coffins. On the north side decaying coffins were visible. Prior to 1829 the churchyard was only one quarter of the current area with room left for very few burials.

With the rapid growth in the population of the Parish – 4,952 in 1851, 6,614 in 1861, 7,861 in 1871, 8,880 in 1881, plus the associated increase in wealth, the church underwent a period of changes. In 1863 major repairs and improvements were carried out. The current pews were installed and the floor renewed, a boiler was installed in the basement of the new North transept and hot water piping distributed around the church under the new floor. The graveyard was extended by purchasing the cottages between the church and the river Bollin, and the Bollin diverted westward onto Glebe land by carting in 6,000 tons of soil. A west doorway and door was constructed as the main church entrance, the current porch was

then used by the priest as a vestry. Other works have come and gone, including the gaslights, the bell ringers' gallery, the Children's Gallery in the north transept, the organ from the West gallery to the East end of the Jesus chapel. The description and accounts of this work by Thomas Clarke, 1866 make good reading. Between 1876 and 1880 the North transept was extended eastwards to create a vestry for the priest, and the porch rebuilt to become the main entrance. In 1898 the Chancel roof was raised, the Clerestory windows installed and new choir stalls fitted. The Children's Gallery in the North transept was removed and the organ moved to its present position. The work was instigated by the Rector, Henry Bates and R.B. Lingard Monk Esq., whose initials can be seen in the ceiling bosses above the screen. The majority of the stained-glass windows were installed during

*The crypt at St Bartholomew's.*

this period and have a significant effect on the appearance of the church. Most of these windows, and also the wall plaques, have dedications and dates thus giving an insight into one part of Parish life.

*Twentieth century*

The fine oak screen for the organ was installed in memory of Harriet Brown (1863-1928). Her interest in cooking and needlework is remembered by the crossed teaspoons and scissors amongst the decorations carved into the border. However, the woodworkers also wanted their skill to be acknowledged and you can find a hammer, chisel and saw in the carvings.

An electric pump was installed for the organ in 1961 and the old manual pump removed, thus freeing the room, which is now used as the Clergy Vestry. Some pre-1961 choirboys who still live in the Parish recall that misbehaviour meant a spell on the organ pump.

In 1979 Mr Emile A. Fadil and his children had the crypt restored in memory of his wife Salwa May Fadil. On its re-opening, the crypt was dedicated as a Chapel of Unity, with three glass panels having the text: 'My Peace I give to you' - John 14.27 in English, Arabic and Hebrew. The east wall of the crypt includes three sedila (seats for clergy in the chancel), which may have been moved to the crypt during rebuilding in 1520.

*Twenty-first century*

Now it is our turn. The main roof beams have worn out and it would be appropriate to have a toilet for the disabled, so we currently have a restoration appeal. Please help. Hopefully work should start in 2003.

R. Franks

# Quarry Bank Mill, Styal: A Family Enterprise, 1784-1959

*The establishment of the Mill*

Samuel Greg was born in Belfast in 1758, the son of Thomas Greg, a Belfast merchant and ship owner, and Elizabeth Hyde, the daughter of a small Lancashire landowner with business interests in the Irish linen trade. He was one of a large family. The economic climate in Northern Ireland at the time was subject to wild fluctuations, and Thomas Greg was prone to suffer through over-speculation in business. In 1766, during one such trade cycle, two of his sons, Thomas and Samuel, were sent to England to be raised by relatives: the former, aged fifteen years, to London and the latter, aged eight years, to Manchester. Both sons seem to have had little contact with their family thereafter.

Samuel Greg was adopted by his childless maternal uncle, Robert Hyde. Upon completing his education, Samuel entered Hyde & Company, one of the largest Manchester based textile merchant-manufacturing businesses, then owned by his uncles, Robert and Nathaniel Hyde, in 1778. Until 1780, he travelled around continental Europe gathering contacts and orders for the firm, before returning to Manchester in 1780 to become a junior partner. In 1782, he became a full partner and later that year, upon the death of Robert Hyde and the retirement of Nathaniel on health grounds, he inherited the company, with a stock valuation of £26,000, and the sum of £10,000 at the age of twenty-four years.

Having gained experience in the textile trade, together with an awareness of the technological advances being made, good contacts and an appreciation that the trade was entering a boom period, Samuel decided that the best way to control his supply of yarn was by owning the unit of production. He was aware of the problems which his uncles had encountered in obtaining a regular supply of good quality yarn for their loom shop in Eyam, Derbyshire, ensuring that they had a sufficient supply of cloth to sell, and thought it was important that he should not suffer in the same manner. With the capital to do so, he began to search for a location where he could build his own cotton spinning mill, eventually coming across a suitable site in Styal.

The local landowner, the Earl of Stamford and Warrington, was willing to lease land, water and building rights to Samuel Greg, and to allow him to use locally-available timber, stone and clay for the construction of his mill. The river Bollin was relatively under-used at Styal, and its water supply was swelled by its tributary, the river Dean, joining the Bollin a short distance upstream from the mill, ensuring that there was sufficient water to power a waterwheel which in turn could power textile machinery. It is likely that building began in late 1783, with production commencing at some point in 1784. Samuel Greg installed machinery necessary to enable him to spin cotton yarn, although not all the processes were powered by water at this time. He estimated that it cost him £16,000 to build and equip the mill, a sum which, he later claimed, nearly ruined him.

## Cotton as a factory industry

The main process, spinning, was the one to transform cotton manufacture from a domestic base to a factory industry. Various inventions had been made in the eighteenth century to speed certain processes, but each time an advance was made, a bottleneck was encountered at some other point in the manufacturing process. In 1769, Richard Arkwright patented the water-frame, the first machine to be built on a scale whereby it could not be accommodated in the domestic setting, and the first to successfully use water as a power source. The water-frame combined previous inventions – Crompton's spinning mule and Hargreaves's spinning jenny - into a single machine – Arkwright's skill being in developing others' inventions and in seeing the entrepreneurial benefits which they would bring to the industry. He was responsible for the first cotton factory in 1771 at Cromford, Derbyshire, and the spread of factories gathered pace over the following decades as others sought to emulate his success.

By the early 1780's, industrialists were increasingly questioning the validity of Arkwright's water-frame patent, wanting to copy the machine without paying patent fees to him. Thus, many mills were built and equipped with copies of water-frames, as was Quarry Bank Mill. In 1785, the patent was finally overthrown, leading to a further expansion in mill building, and the re-equipping of existing mills with authentic water-frames, including Quarry Bank.

## The Mill's workforce

As an agrarian hamlet of isolated farmsteads and outbuildings, Styal could not provide Samuel Greg's new mill with a workforce of sufficient size. However, there was some tradition of local handicraft work to supplement seasonal agricultural employment, backing buttons for the Macclesfield silk industry and handloom weaving for the Yorkshire woollen industry.

In the early years of the Mill, up to a half of the workforce were child apprentices, offered to the Mill by the Parish Overseers of Newcastle-under-Lyme, Liverpool, East Anglia, South Cheshire, Middlesex and beyond. As their employer, Greg had responsibility for the board and lodging, clothing, education and religious instruction of his apprentice workforce, whom he indentured to serve him for a number of years from the age of nine. Adult workers were recruited from the surrounding area.

As the Mill expanded, so it required a larger workforce. Initially, farm outbuildings were converted into housing but once this supply had been exhausted, a programme of building to a high standard began in the early 1800's. By 1823, a community identity had begun to appear, with a shop, Baptist (later Unitarian) chapel and school available for villagers. This expanded during the course of the century to include a Methodist chapel, beerhouse, butcher and public house. A Sick Club and Burial, Female, Mutual Improvement and Debating Societies were also established for the benefit of the community.

Although harsh by today's standards, working conditions were favourable when compared to the experiences suffered in other mills and industries, with the Mill's employees having the added benefits of a rural location bringing with it a healthier environment and diet. The standard of living of Mill employees was higher than that of those living in the emerging industrial towns and cities of the North West.

At its peak, the Mill employed 454 people. It persevered with the apprentice system until no longer able to do so by law in 1847, unlike the majority of other mills where it was less common after 1820 because it was cheaper to employ free labour.

*More power for the Mill*

Quarry Bank Mill quickly became a very profitable enterprise, and by 1796 Samuel Greg had accumulated enough capital, and was confident enough about his future business prospects, to embark upon an expansion of the Mill buildings. The floor area and machinery in the Mill was expanded by 50%, with a second waterwheel added to power the extra machinery, along with improvements to the supply of water by 1801, including a stone weir.

In 1796, Samuel Greg entered into a business partnership with Peter Ewart, the latter bringing technological experience to the firm, complimenting Greg's entrepreneurial skills. It was Ewart who oversaw the expansion of the Mill, the rationalisation of the machinery and the improvements to the power systems. He had previously served an apprenticeship at the Boulton and Watt works in Birmingham before acting as their Northern agent, and had some practical experience of the cotton industry gained from a short-lived partnership with Samuel Oldknow at Stockport in 1792 – 1793.

By 1810, Ewart realised that the water supply to the Mill was not sufficiently reliable for the latter to be able to operate at full capacity for sustained periods throughout the year. To overcome this, he introduced a supplementary power source, a small steam engine acquired from Boulton & Watt, to take some of the burden off the waterwheels. Steam power was increasingly relied upon throughout the rest of the Mill's manufacturing life.

Between 1816 and 1822, a further phase of Mill expansion saw the building of a new block housing a much more powerful waterwheel. The wheel, of the high breast-shot suspension type designed and built by Thomas Hewes, was much larger than previous wheels at the Mill, which it replaced, with the valley being surveyed to allow more water to flow to and from the wheel to provide the maximum amount of power to drive the machinery.

*New technology*

The Mill was constantly experimenting with new machinery to boost productivity, either replacing existing machines or introducing new processes. Some of the trials were successful and implemented at the Mill, others were of benefit to the other mills in the Greg enterprise acquired from 1817, and some were abandoned as inappropriate. One trial which was to have a profound impact upon the later development of the Mill was power loom weaving, introduced in 1823.

Although invented by Dr Cartwright in 1785, the power loom was unreliable and not widely adopted within the industry until the 1820's, by which time it had been improved. The trials at Quarry Bank were quite successful and weaving was introduced to some of the other family mills but not to Quarry Bank until after Samuel Greg's death in 1834.

*Samuel Greg: his legacy*

Samuel was fortunate to have the capital available to invest in his own business at a time when the cotton industry was expanding rapidly, with a largely untapped home market and the prospect of further expansion overseas once this had been satisfied. The costs of building and technology, although not insubstantial, were low in comparison to the later stages of industrialisation, and the demands for a skilled workforce were similarly reduced. He had the knowledge, contacts and the foresight to speculate, and was handsomely rewarded for the risks taken.

He oversaw the expansion of a family enterprise to encompass five mills by the time of his death, employing over 2,000 people and producing 0.6% of all the world's yarn and 1.03% of all cloth. This was at a time when there were many mills in existence, but they were mainly small in size. He had amassed a personal fortune of £312,000, and enjoyed a privileged social status through his wealth, mixing with many of the most eminent members of North West society.

*A new figurehead for the Mill: Robert Hyde Greg*

Robert Hyde Greg was born in Manchester in 1795, and was the first of Samuel's sons to enter the family business in 1817 as a junior partner. He did not enjoy the best of relationships with his father, having more in common with the broader interests of his mother. Upon his father's death, he took control of the business, managing the partnership, Quarry Bank Mill and the Greg Brothers marketing concern in Manchester until 1841, when the partnership was dissolved to allow each brother to manage their own mill.

It was Robert Hyde Greg who oversaw the introduction of weaving at Quarry Bank, with the building of weaving sheds alongside the river from 1836. Under his management, the Mill continued to expand with the construction of additional buildings, a gas plant for lighting and further steam engines and boilers. He was, however, unfortunate in that the industry was no longer able to sustain the spectacular growth rates it had experienced during his father's lifetime, and he continually had to strive to sustain its profitability and suffered from poor health as a consequence.

He was also an influential figure within the industry and North West society, becoming one of the first Members of Parliament for Manchester between 1839–1841, elected as a supporter of the Anti-Corn Law League. After stepping down from Parliament, he continued to lobby on issues relating to the industry, in particular arguing against legislation restricting the hours of work of employees in textile factories and seeking exemption for those owning water-powered mills.

Unlike his father, he was able to pursue outside interests to a far greater degree, being a keen horticulturist responsible for designing and planting Norcliffe Hall gardens and surrounding woodlands with exotic, non-indigenous species.

*Beyond Styal: the growth and decline of the family business*
Robert Hyde Greg also built the Albert and Victoria Mills on his estate in Reddish in 1847, running the former until 1858 before allowing it to pass to another son, Henry Russell Greg and leasing the latter.

He oversaw a period of unsettled times in the enterprise, with two of his younger brothers, Samuel Junior and William Rathbone Greg, not being competent businessmen and getting their mills into financial difficulties in Bollington and Bury respectively, both leaving the firm by 1850 to embark upon alternative careers. Only his brother John, managing the mills at Lancaster and Caton, was suited to business,

and when he retired in 1864, only the Quarry Bank and Albert Mills were retained.

Like his father who built a family residence at Quarry Bank House, Robert Hyde also chose to live in Styal, building Norcliffe Hall in 1829 for his growing family.

*The later years*
Robert Hyde Greg retired from the firm in 1870 to be succeeded by his son, Edward Hyde Greg, the latter overseeing operations until 1900. Edward Hyde was not particularly interested in the business, enjoying the prestige which manufacturing wealth had brought to his family, and had the misfortune to enter an antiquated mill in decline within a troubled industry increasingly challenged by foreign competition.

By 1880, the Mill was making an annual loss as the market for coarse yarn was particularly badly affected, and orders began to dry up. By 1894, the Mill ceased its spinning operations on economic grounds after 110 years, concentrating instead upon weaving.

In 1900, Robert Alexander Greg took over from his father and began a programme of modernization in an attempt to revitalise the Mill's fortunes and ensure its survival. Water turbines replaced the waterwheel by 1905. He ran the Mill until 1923 when, with his brother, Ernest William, and other members of the family, he converted it into a limited company, the family remaining principal shareholders. By the 1930's, the Mill was unable to weave calico economically, switching to making laundry bags, which continued until the Mill's eventual closure in 1959 after 175 years production.

*Postscript: National Trust and Museum*
In 1939, Ernest William's son, Alexander Carlton, donated the Mill, village and estate to the National Trust to prevent land being used for housing. After its closure, parts of the Mill buildings were sub-let whilst others were left to deteriorate. By the late 1960's, major repairs were required to preserve the buildings. Eventually, the idea to develop the Mill into a museum of the cotton industry gathered momentum, and the first visitors were admitted in 1978.

Further developments saw the Museum's reputation prosper, winning numerous awards. In July 2000, management transferred to the National Trust, re-uniting the estate under a single body.

*Adam Daber – Curator, Quarry Bank Mill*
*(National Trust)*

# Before your time: other people's memories of the Rex cinema, Wilmslow

The Rex, Alderley Road, opened on 15 October 1936, with 876 seats. It has been used for live theatre, and was reduced to 328 seats in 1994. Closed June 1995, it later became a bookshop, the Book Gallery, owned by Mr Paul Stansby, and is currently a furniture store.

The Book Gallery. I used to work there.

'Have you got any books on Doris Day? She was one of my favourites, Doris Day. I saw all her pictures. Saw them here.'

'I remember the first night. *The Charge of the Light Brigade* with Errol Flynn and Olivia de Havilland. You'll not know them. Before your time'.

### THE REX OPENING PROGRAMME

Thursday October 15 1936
Formal Opening of the Theatre
by Mrs Walter Bromley-Davenport

Errol Flynn – Olivia de Havilland
Basil Rathbone
in *Captain Blood*

### FORTHCOMING ATTRACTIONS

Monday, Tuesday and Wednesday
October 19 to 21 1936
Jessie Matthews – Sonnie Hale
in *First Girl*

Thursday, Friday and Saturday
October 22 to 24 1936
Fred Astaire – Ginger Rogers
in *Follow the Fleet*

'I love your stairs. I can just imagine Fred Astaire and Ginger Rogers dancing up and down those stairs. And Gene Kelly. I don't know about Ray Bolger. I'm not sure about him. I'd have to think.'

'I'd just had all my teeth out. My bottom teeth. Oh, I thought, to hell with it. I'll go to the Rex. It's Margaret Lockwood. That'll take my mind off. So I'm sat there. I've just sat down. I've got this taste in my mouth. This peculiar taste. It's blood. I'm bleeding. There's blood all down my front. So I go home and ring the dentist. He's at a Freemason's dinner and he'll not be back till midnight. So I have to sit up until midnight. Then walk all the way to the surgery. And I never did get to see Margaret Lockwood.'

'I saw them all at the Rex. All the big names. Anthony Quayle, Eric Sykes, Anna Neagle. Anna Neagle gave me her

*The Rex buildings. (Courtesy* Wilmslow Express)

autograph. I've still got it somewhere. I used to like her in all those films she did with Michael Wilding. Spring in Park Lane, Maytime in Mayfair, The Courtneys of Curzon Street. Those days'll never come back. I'm sorry to say.'

'There was this old lady. I don't know who she was, I never knew her name, but you'd see her at the front, knitting. Always knitting. She had this laugh. If Abott and Costello were on, you'd hear her. You'd know she was there. Every time I see Abbott and Costello I think of her. Even now.'

'I never liked it here. Couldn't be doing with it. My wife and I always went to the Majestic'.

'You've missed her again', said Helen (the manager). 'That lady who used to be one of the usherettes. She was telling me all about it'.

'Have you got or can you get *The Keys of the Kingdom* by A.J. Cronin? It's not for me, it's for my sister. She saw the film years ago. I think she saw it here. Gregory Peck was in it. Big fan of his, my sister. She went to see *The Snows of Kilimanjaro* three times. I couldn't stick him, Gregory Peck, couldn't stick him. Even in *The Guns of Navarone*. No luck? When you say out of print, does

# REX THEATRE

### WILMSLOW

Large Car Park    **Advance Booking Tel. Wilmslow 22266 & 24850**    Theatre Bar

### ON THE STAGE

## Week commencing MONDAY, JANUARY 19th, 1970

MONDAY to FRIDAY at 8 p.m.     SATURDAY at 6 and 8.40 p.m.

PRICES: 14/6, 12/6, 10/6, 8/3.

### MICHAEL WHITE

presents

# ANTHONY QUAYLE
# KEITH BAXTER

in

# SLEUTH

## A New Thriller by
## ANTHONY SHAFFER

## Directed by CLIFFORD WILLIAMS

## Designed by CARL TOMS

## Lighting by FRANCIS REID

# Opening London February 12th, 1970

ECHO PRESS LTD., LOUGHBOROUGH

*Flyer promoting* Sleuth, *showing at the Rex Theatre, 1970.*

that mean you can't get it? I told her. Told her. But no. She wouldn't have it. As usual. She'll just have to have *The Snows of Kilimanjaro*. Who wrote that?'

'The Welshman. Stanley Baker. He was in it. Harry Andrews. And Theodore Bikel. Not Theodore Bikel. Yes. Theodore Bikel. The three of them. In the desert. It was terrible. One of the worst films I've ever seen. I know I was on my own in here that day. Had the place to myself. The only time it ever happened to me. King of the Rex'.

'The last one I saw here was…what was it? *The Madness of King George*. That was it. No, it wasn't. It was that other one. What was it? First time I've ever forgotten. I'll tell you in a minute'.

Owing to Adverse Trading conditions the book gallery has ceased to be commercially viable and the store will be closing on Saturday May 19 2001. From June Multiyork Furnishings will begin to establish their business at these premises.

P. Stansby

'What's Paul going to do with himself, then? Is he off to France? What about you and Helen? What's the name again? MulitYork? Never heard of them. It was bad enough when the Rex shut down. The times I've been there. I couldn't tell you. Couldn't begin to tell you'.

On the wall of the MultiYork Ltd Hangs a framed photograph: The Rex Theatre and Buildings, Wilmslow. 'Before your Time'. Now showing: Edmond O'Brien in *The Killers*. 1946. Before my time.

*Liam Kerrigan*

# Twenty years in the life of The Greyhound, Handforth

When my parents moved into The Greyhound Hotel on Wilmslow Road in Handforth, the large papier mache decorations from Queen Elizabeth II's Coronation were still in the garages, and the asbestos huts, making up 61 M.U. (Second World War installation), were still opposite on the old village green.

The year was 1954, and my parents, Arthur and Alex Henley-Smith, were excited (and nervous) about going into business in their own public house as tenants (which meant they were tied to a brewery, but made profit for themselves, and not just the brewery), rather than managers, as they had been in their previous pubs in Rochdale and Chorlton.

The Greyhound, now demolished and replaced with an apartment building,a had been a coaching inn for many years, and was reputed to be the first stop for changing horses en-route from Manchester to London along the old A34, and it was still a bus stop all the time we lived there.

The façade of The Greyhound, at that time, was black and white with an added balcony across the front. I have heard it described as '1920's Mock Tudor', but think that some of the black and white effect was done in the Victorian era, as 'At the sign of Greyhound' was a coach stop in Handforth (as Handforth was then called) when it was sold by auction in 1816. There was a small private garden at the rear and an immaculately-kept large crown bowling green, with narrow flower beds on all four sides of it. My mother was the gardener and she soon had roses, honeysuckle, Lupins, and all manner of colourful plants in the flower beds. The greensman, Jim England,

*The Greyhound Hotel as it was in 1954 when Alex and Arthur Henley-Smith took it over.*

kept the bowling green in pristine order, sometimes mowing every day – a job that was done with a push-mower back then. Mr England was a very fit man!

There was a separate, dark panelled, dining room, (which seemed very large to me in those days, but which could only seat about forty people in a formal setting) which soon became the place in the village to have wedding receptions, christening parties and funeral teas, and which looked rather splendid when the tables were laid up with pristine white cloths, shiny cutlery, silver epergnes with flowers and trailing greenery. Cooked lunches were served to the local businessmen in here on weekdays

(only sandwiches were served in the bar areas), and coach parties of people came from Manchester to have a Bowls Match, a chicken dinner and a sing-song with the pianist in the Concert Room, and then taken safely back to Manchester again.

As children, my brother Anthony, and I, were never allowed in the public bar areas during opening hours, which by today's standards were quite short – 11 a.m.–3 p.m., and 5.30 p.m.–10.30 p.m., Monday to Saturday, and 12 noon–2 p.m., and 7 p.m.–10 p.m. on Sundays. No children were allowed in the bar at all!

Although my Father did employ cleaners, a cook, bar staff and (on Fridays and

*The Greyhound Hotel, Handforth, decorated for the Coronation of King George IV, 1936.*

*Entrance to the Victoria public house*

Saturdays) waiting-on staff, Mum and Dad did a full day's work as the fill-in cleaners, the kitchen assistants, the extra cellar man, those responsible for stock replenishment, the book-keeper and cashier, the buyers of food and extra stock that wasn't delivered direct, as well as looking after my brother and myself and our living quarters upstairs 'above the shop'.

It was a fantastic place for a child to live. Masses of corridors to run around in, plenty of secure space outside to ride our bikes around in, large living quarters that went up two steps then down three (where the building had been extended) and just a short distance from Wilmslow for shopping and the cinema, and, as we got older, youth club and operatic society.

The pub had a darts team, a domino team, a bowls team – and my Mother and Father supported them all. There were numerous photographs in the local newspapers of trophy presentations to the victorious teams.

Sunday lunchtimes in the pub had a special feel to them. My Mother put bowls of crisps and nuts and pieces of cheese and crispy bacon bits along the bars, and I used to be allowed to help with this and then perhaps meet some of the customers who came in for a drink before going home to their Sunday roast. One of my friends tells me that it was special for her too, as she was brought along by her Grandfather on Sunday lunchtimes, and she sat outside in the sunshine by the bowling green and was allowed a packet of crisps (always Smith's Potato Crisps with the salt in a twist of blue paper) and an orange squash – gentle days.

*Mrs S. Riley*

# The Quaker Meeting House in Wilmslow

In the seventeenth century, Quakers in the Wilmslow area were, as throughout the country, classed as Dissenters. They were therefore prohibited from having a Meeting House, meetings of more than four people were illegal and, as well as being liable to be arrested, they were fined for refusing to pay tithes to the Church. However, they did meet in various homes until the Toleration Act of 1689 allowed them to have a Meeting House.

For this purpose, they obtained the lease of a house at Morley, a mile and a half from the centre of Wilmslow, along the Altrincham Road, which they used until the lease was due to expire in 1829. It was near a path that led across the fields from Styal. They had also acquired land in Mobberley for a burial ground, which was used until 1848. Graveyard Lane in Mobberley still bears its name.

On the expiry of the existing leases, the Morley Meeting of the Society of Friends acquired a paddock at the western outskirts of Wilmslow town, on what was then all open country. There they built a new Meeting House, first used in 1831. It was a substantial brick building, in design typical of contemporary Quaker meeting houses, with two large, high rooms on either side of the central passageway. The paddock sloped down from the back of the building, and a short distance down they also built a single-storey carriage shed with stabling for six horses. Support for the Meeting had long been among local farmers and agricultural workers and their families; hence provision for carts and carriages would be a necessity. In Victorian times, this need would be increased, with the expansion of Wilmslow and Alderley Edge bringing many town dwellers of the same persuasion and using horse-drawn vehicles to get to the Meeting. A lane running down from Altrincham Road gave access by a wide gate into the paddock. Later in the nineteenth century, this lane became Bourne Street, with houses built as far as Simpson Street. A burial ground was located to the east of the Meeting House.

Fifty years later, the Quakers undertook further building. By this time the Adult School movement was active across the country and the local Quakers participated in the widespread nineteenth-century work of teaching people, both children and adults, to read and write. In order to accommodate increasing numbers it was decided to build a second storey on top of the carriage shed. This was a typically economical project, using the existing

building as a base. A door was opened on Bourne Street, to lead to a staircase to the schoolroom. This entry can still be recognised in a bricked-up arched doorway, with a built-in roundel 'Friends Meeting House'. Opened in 1883, the schoolroom was intended to accommodate up to 200 students, and an offshoot area above part of the stables was called the Infants' schoolroom; it had stepped benches around two walls.

Changing times again brought changing needs. State schools were opened; and wartime conditions and the partial enfranchisement of women altered the expectations of women by 1920. Also, Wilmslow was expanding steadily. The schoolroom was used less and less, especially during the week.

Two members of the Wilmslow Meeting were to be instrumental in changing the use

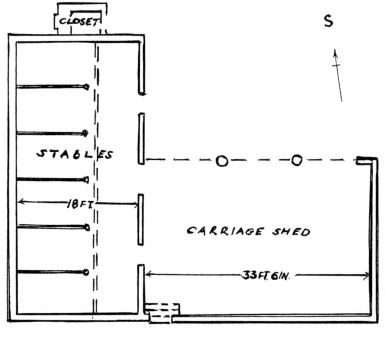

*Illustration of the floor plan for the Meeting House stables and carriage shed. (Courtesy M. Oughton)*

and shape of the schoolroom forever. Maud and Russell Brayshaw, both of them committed to adult education, were founder members of Wilmslow Beacon Guild in 1926, which was allowed to use the schoolroom for classes and music and drama performances on lease from the Meeting. The schoolroom was 57ft by 21ft, with a wall height of 9ft 6ins. It was not ceiled but open above the beams to the underside of the slated roof. Beneath it, the carriage shed was open at the front. Therefore the schoolroom was always a chilly meeting place, even though various attempts were made to improve conditions by installing boilers in the cellar space under the stable area. The Infants' Room, about 16ft square, served a whole range of needs: Guild Warden's office, adult classroom, costume storage area and annex to the stage.

The earliest dramatic and musical presentations were performed on a stage of large beams of railway sleeper dimensions laid across the tops of Sunday School forms. Quakers and Guild alike were nothing if not inventive. In time the open front of the carriage shed was enclosed with wooden screens and doors, becoming a scenery and property store for the Guild Players. After the Guild was able to construct its own building in 1963 – by leasing a large part of the paddock – the schoolroom saw further changes, with the construction of a stage and proscenium and raked seating. The low height up to the beams could cause problems for tall players – they had to be careful about the height of any headgear – and the stage area was very cramped. Nothing could be done about the acoustics of the vault of the pitched roof and meeting fire and safety requirements presented

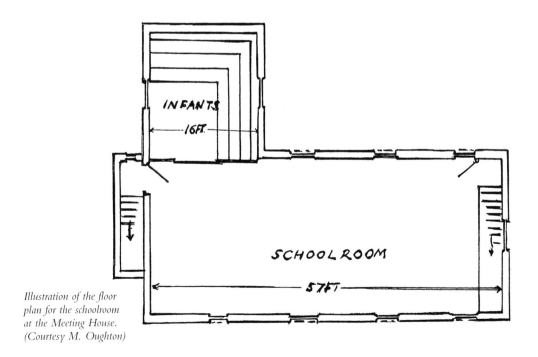

*Illustration of the floor plan for the schoolroom at the Meeting House. (Courtesy M. Oughton)*

problems. Nevertheless the schoolroom was transformed into a creditable intimate theatre seating some eighty to ninety people. So intimate was it that there were notices in the dressing room in the former stables below the stage area which ordered that toilets were not to be flushed during performances!

Other Guild Groups gradually took up other parts of the building; the photographic group had a darkroom in the old stable area, and in the 1980s one of the dressing rooms in the same area was shared with Manchester, Salford and District Hospital Radio as a recording studio for making tapes. Needless to say in these cramped conditions, there was some conflict of interests over storage and cleaning. Quaker use of the building was almost nil.

Those who attended performances by the Guild Players will remember entering the 'auditorium' via the door off Bourne Street and the narrow steep stairs. Those stairs had seen a succession of 'names' as the years passed. One, in the late 1920s, was pianist Edward Isaacs, highly respected in Manchester musical circles. The programme for the event made special note of the fact that a Steinway grand piano would be used, size not stated; one wonders how a grand piano was manoeuvred up that narrow staircase into the schoolroom. Wartime brought several players who achieved later note – Doris Speed, Violet Carson and, later, a young Albert Finney. The schoolroom became therefore a theatre until the Meeting was forced to terminate its lease in the late 1980s.

The fine Meeting House was gradually swallowed up by residential buildings as Wilmslow expanded westwards. The name Morley Meeting was used until the early 1960s, when it became Wilmslow Meeting. The Meeting House itself in due time became a Listed Building Grade II* and in the 1980s the members of the Meeting realised the need for extensive repairs and modifications to their building. Costs being beyond their immediate assets, various plans were formulated to raise necessary finance, such as sheltered housing partially within the schoolhouse, or specialist offices completely in that building, but all failed to secure planning permission. In the end a scheme was devised to sell the Meeting House and part of the land (including the adjacent burial ground, no longer used) for internal conversion to a number of office suites. As the building remained listed, its exterior could not be altered.

Although the Meeting House of 1831 now houses a number of commercial offices, it remains probably the most significant of Wilmslow's older architectural prizes, still presenting its nineteenth-century face to the traffic on Altrincham Road from behind a screen of great trees that include massive beeches and a handsome cedar of Lebanon. On the other hand, the schoolroom – intimate theatre for about thirty years – was transformed, for it became the new Meeting House, used for Meeting for Worship for the first time on 21 May 1995. Now an elegant building both inside and out, with all the theatrical trappings gone, it has been transformed imaginatively and appropriately to the modern size of the meeting, The Meeting Room itself soars from ground level over most of the original carriage shed up to the roof, providing a tranquil place some 18ft high, lit chiefly by the old upper-storey windows well above the sight lines of those who meet for quiet worship. This building also retains its listed status Grade II as part of the cartilage of the original Meeting House.

Those Quakers who put up the carriage shed in 1831 could have little anticipated such structural changes, or thought of the unlikely stream of people who would pass through it during the next 150 years. They might sigh with silent thankfulness at the appropriateness of its final design and ambiance as their modern successors conduct their quiet worship on ground originally reserved for carriages and horses.

*Marguerita Oughton*
*With acknowledgements to the Society of Friends*
*Wilmslow Meeting.*

# 7 Leisure

## The chronicles of the WOSA

Mr Heppleston, headmaster of Wilmslow Modern School, Wycliffe Avenue, founded the Wilmslow Old Scholars' Association on 6 March 1929, according to WOSA's first magazine in 1939. In a message from the General Secretary, Mr H. Ainsworth, it was said: 'The Educational Authorities kindly provide the surroundings, and the WOSA's are jolly good mixers, so please send the youngsters along and I'll do the rest'.

They held a meeting every week in the 1930s in the Modern School. Events arranged were: outings and social events, tennis in the school playground, supper dances in the Rex Ballroom costing only two shillings. The Rambling Section was an 'outing' and a revue was a social event.

Eileen has kept the log of their walks in 1937 and 1938, and as a result of exploring my family history, she loaned me these two books. The following excerpts are priceless in illustrating the mood and culture of the day. All the participants were young people who walked eighteen to twenty miles for pleasure.

### 'RAMBLE 2 SHUTTLINGSLOW'

'A memorable day was spent on Sunday May 23rd, rambling over the hills and moors. After catching the 9.30 a.m. bus to Macclesfield, (Kathleen caught it by steaming through Grove Street at thirty miles per hour just as the bus came along) we struck out over the Macclesfield Golf Links, and so up the hill and down the dale until we reached Tegg's Nose, which in itself is a hill of precipitous nature near some quarries. Eileen, the leader of the Ramble, (who up till now had been near the back of the party) was feeling a new attack of energy, and so decided to put into practice the fact that the shortest distance between two points was a straight line, and so down Tegg's nose she went, followed by Allen, the rest of the party continuing in a more sure-footed and comfortable way, albeit perhaps apparently a little further. Nevertheless, we were sitting down at the bottom eating fruit while Eileen and Allen were still scrambling on their downward climb, for Old Tegg had a few more curves and joints in his nose than they had anticipated. From this vantage point we had a glorious view of the surrounding district, Langley Reservoir lay below us. Far distant amongst the hills was Shuttlingsloe which we were destined to see from North, South, East and West, before we finished our 'walk'. The sun, up until now, had been clothing nature in its Sunday suit, as it were, everything looked so beautiful.

After resting a little longer, (for Eileen and Allen were both ready for as long a respite as time would allow) we continued through a small wood, (which we learnt afterwards was a reserve for game) and so to the side of the reservoir and on to the main road again. There we encountered a heavy shower of rain which, however, finished as soon as some of us had got our mackintoshes on. On and on we tramped, along what seemed a never-ending road, until the Hanging Gate Inn was reached, and very much welcomed, for dinner was indicated. Before dinner, Allen and Tom refreshed themselves with a bottle of mineral water each, which they had brought with them. Tom Steele, the proprietor of the inn, proceeded to brew tea for us. Here let me say that Mr Steele had only one arm, and I afterwards learned that he quite enjoyed washing up. We also learnt from Mr Steele that buses in the district came twice a week – Friday and Saturday.

The weather had now nearly completely changed, and with grey overhanging clouds and intermittent rain (which we experienced until tea time) we went past Greenway Cross at the southern end of Wildboarclough. Greenway Cross is the place reputed to be where food, goods and money were exchanged in the time of the Plague.

We were now walking along the road again, and winding our way we plodded on, it was now raining quite hard, until we came to the turn over the moors again to Three Shires Bridge. Here we rested awhile, and at the same time admired the beauty of the surrounds. Three Shires Bridge is the junction of Cheshire, Derbyshire and Staffordshire.

Let it suffice to say that we now continued over the moors to the Cat & Fiddle for tea, another meal everyone was ready for. The last stage of the journey was mainly along the road from the Cat & Fiddle to Macclesfield. The only deviation from the road was across a field containing about a dozen cows.

Macclesfield was heralded once more, as ten of us approached and only a little while later boarded the bus to Wilmslow.

The 'ten' were: Nancy, Joan (Broadhurst), Sheila, Eileen, Kathleen, Jessie, Fred, Tom, Allan and Ada.

*(Written by G.F. Camm)*

Sadly the events of 1939 and following years took their toll. Many members lost their lives, others moved away, some emigrated, and others remained locally. One couple look forward to their diamond wedding celebration in September 2002.

*Carole Holmes*

# Fifty years of shopping, shipping and Shakespeare

There's been some mention in the local press recently of de-pedestrianising Grove Street. What a good idea. Could it be a first step towards revitalising the place?

When we arrived here, as the first half of the twentieth century was closing, there was two-way traffic in Grove Street and all the shops were open. In those days shopping was almost entirely in proper shops, rather than in supermarkets and uniformly-fronted chain stores that have sucked the character out of high streets up and down the country. There were three grocers shops: T. Seymour Mead and Burgoyne's, both in Grove Street, and Tomlinson's in Water Lane, where you could find items that the others didn't stock. There was a pork butcher's shop, Chadwick's, in Grove Street, as well as a branch of Dewhurst's – general butchers –

further down. Greengroceries were supplied by Jackson's on the corner of Water Lane. Owen's wine shop, a warm, traditional family business remained until the '80s and had cellars that extended the width of Grove Street. The 'young' Mr Owen would make an annual pilgrimage to the wine-growing regions of France to select his vintages in person; they were eventually taken over by Peter Dominic.

Another long established family business is Charnley's chemist shop, which weathered the arrival of Boots much further down the street without any apparent inconvenience.

Seeing Grove Street now, pedestrianised, with banks and building societies, a café wine bar and fly-by-night enterprises that come and go like April showers, it's hard to believe that it was once a bustling thoroughfare with businesses rooted in the town's own foundations; when you could take your pony and trap to Bourne's back entrance in Green Lane to buy a couple of sacks of corn for the horse, and have him shod by the farrier next door while you went through the front for a call on W. Hyslop a few doors away to top up on a variety of equine tack. Berry's gents' outfitters, Edith Dennett's dress shop, Johnstone's book shop, Kellett's ironmongers and the British Workman's Mission – all vanished. There's nowhere now to buy a decent pipe or have your personal blend made up from a shelf of glass jars full of Virginia, Latakia, Cavendish and many other tobaccos that allegedly shorten your life, but help to make what's left of it more tolerable – Hardcastle's used to provide all that and anything else the dedicated pipe-man desired.

The largest shop in the village was

*The Norfolk family at Fulshaw Hall – 1954.*

*Charnley's pharmacy.*

Clegg's, standing foursquare on the corner of Hawthorn Lane and Church Street. It was a household department store selling furniture, bed and table linen, curtains, carpets and kitchenware. White & Swales was the main record shop, but, for sheet music, pianos, mouth organs, piccolos, clarinets, trombones, euphoniums and a myriad of other instruments, you'd have to visit Music in Station Road. This was Mr Gamble's establishment, a place where violins were not only repaired but also made. On Water Lane you'd find Rathbone's monumental mason's yard, long

ago replaced by a car salesroom, and Finnegan's (now Hooper's) had not yet been built, and where the Lloyds TSB now stands there was a handsome white-painted Georgian house stood on a low knoll, which we considered the most attractive dwelling in the area.

As I write, the Rex is now a furniture store, but back then it was the more salubrious of two cinemas in the village – the other was the Palace, near the train station. As well as films the Rex offered live theatre, with professional touring companies presenting plays with famous names in the

121

*Show jumper Pat Smythe competing at the Wilmslow Horse Show, 1956.*

*A dry Lindow Lake, 1976.*

cast like Jack Hulbert and Gerald Harper. The Wilmslow Operatic Society also staged shows there, and later the East Cheshire, while every year Chris Paling produced a lavish pantomime during a week of the Christmas holidays.

While the Rex catered for the big stage productions the smaller amateur dramatics societies played in more economical venues – the Wilmslow A.D.S. at the Parish Hall and then in Water Lane, opposite the end of Kennerley's Lane, in a building long ago demolished and replaced by offices. The Guild Players had their own theatre in Bourne Street and to reach the stage from the dressing room you had to cross part of an open courtyard – on a chill winters eve with a north-easterly blowing round your Shakespearean tights your ardour could be somewhat cooled!

The Green Room, then as now, was an amateur society with a professional outlook. They played at the old public Hall, but since Safeways took over the site they have created their own theatre in Chapel Lane. They were, probably, the only amateur dramatic as opposed to operatic company, to play at the Rex with Peter Ustinov's *The Love of Four Colonels*.

An exciting feature during the '50s was the Wilmslow Horse Show, this originally took place on the Rectory Field, now occupied by the leisure centre, but it soon outgrew that venue and transferred to the Rugby Club. Several household names in the world of show-jumping were seen there – Colonel Harry Llewellyn with Foxhunter, a horse that became a legend in the sport, Pat Smythe – a young David Broome, Ted Edgar and many more.

Lindow Common was livelier in those times, before it suffered the kiss of death when it was designated a 'Site of Special Scientific Interest'. Horse riders and cyclists would meander along the wooded path, access was unrestricted allowing you right up to the waters edge, and children would fish in the Black Lake – although I never heard of anyone ever catching anything – except during the freezing winter of 1962/63 when the lake was frozen solid and the skaters came out in force, and in the searing summer of 1976 when the green pastures of England were scorched brown and the lake, perhaps for the first time in living memory, was completely dry.

In the 1960's and '70s a stroll to Lindow on a fine Sunday morning was particularly rewarding. Model boat builders used to come from far and wide to show off their craft, and a wonderful variety could be found there. Yachts, cruisers, cargo ships, speedboats and experimental hulls with power units but no superstructure, provided an intriguing, entertaining show for anyone who came to see – and many did. There were craft driven by wind, steam, diesel and electricity, owners in slacks, shorts or long waders in case their beloved vessels should get caught up in the weeds or reeds far out from shore. The undoubted star was a steam-driven tugboat about thirty inches long, slow in its progress through the water, but perfect in every detail of its structure and fittings. It was radio-controlled, and manoeuvred to port or starboard with the precision of a full-scale original. It could even go astern and the acknowledging tinkle of the engine room telegraph would float across the ripples as the Captain, standing on the bank with his little black box, issued orders for 'Full ahead', 'Half speed astern' and, at the end of the voyage, 'Finished with engines'. It was a sad day for the young, and the young at heart, when the council banned the sailing of model boats on the lake and turned it into a bird sanctuary. It's certainly hard to deny that some of the diesel-powered speedboats kicked up a racket distressful to the peace-loving inhabitants of Racecourse Road, but it would have been kinder to have passed a bye-law excluding those nuisances while continuing to welcome the wind, steam and battery powered craft that gave nothing but delight to all who saw them.

Village characters have deliberately not been mentioned in this piece, as it would be discourteous of an incomer of barely fifty-two years' standing, such as myself, to comment on them…okay then, perhaps just one! There was an elderly gentleman, generously paunched, who was in the habit of promenading the streets on hot summer days attired only in khaki shorts and sandals. One sweltering afternoon my wife and I were walking along Kennerley's Lane with our three-year-old daughter running on ahead. Suddenly she spotted this vision of dignified corpulence approaching along the opposite pavement, stopped dead, right-turned with a Guardsman's precision, and pointed at him with arm and finger as rigid as a bowman's arrow: 'Wot's datz!!?' she demanded.

*Tim Norfolk*

# Carnival memories – Wilmslow carnival (1930-1939)

Wilmslow Carnival was held for many years up to 1939, when the Second World War caused its cessation. The 1st of July each year was the date aimed for, and dependant on the Saturday nearest to that date, would be the day reserved for a Carnival, which was generally hailed as 'the best in the area'.

A procession would form up at a designated start point, often a large field or meadow within a quarter to one mile of Wilmslow centre, and progress along the main roads of Wilmslow – Altrincham Road, Hawthorn Street, Chapel Lane, Alderley Road, Green Lane, Bank Square, Grove Street, Water Lane – finishing at the 'Carnival Field' near Lindow Common.

A Carnival Committee organized the day. The committee consisted of various council staff, shopkeepers of Wilmslow, councillors, and the police, who would have a presence so as to prepare traffic policy.

Dozens of farm carts (flat ones with tableaus built on them) drawn by Shire horses, and manned by the farmers themselves; milk floats with Cobs pulling them; and by the 1930's motor vehicles (again flat wagons, so that they could be decorated), took part in the procession, as did steam engines pulling lorries; fire engines (old ones pulled by horse and cart, and other old ones from other villages, pulled by firemen), and coal merchants wagons advertising their services. Between thirty and fifty floats would take part, as did the local shops, bicycle delivery boys of every trade, alongside the local coach company Banks, and Fox, a taxi firm. Every float would have a different theme from weddings to Robin Hood, Red Cross to St John's Ambulance, pantomimes to hospitals, so many different styles that over the years the list would be endless.

Being in late June to July, many, many flowers, vegetables and fruit would be available and were freely given by the traders, farmers and private gardens so as to decorate the floats, the horse harnesses, canopies, wheels and cycles.

The Carnival day was probably the most important occasion after Christmas or Easter bank holiday, so everybody who could, joined in, or lined the procession route to cheer as the procession passed. It was run as a charity event in aid of hospitals generally, but in particular for Alderley Cottage Hospital, which was our own local hospital to which the doctor would send you first before they, the hospital, sent you to Macclesfield or Knutsford or South Manchester hospitals if they were not equipped to deal with your particular problem. Volunteer collectors would walk alongside the procession rattling their collecting boxes, or the floats would hold out sheets for coins to be thrown into them. Very valuable contributions were collected from this daylong event.

At the Carnival Field, where the procession ended, there would be beer and refreshment tents, Punch and Judy, Aunt Sally shy stalls, ducking stool stalls, sponge throwing (sometimes someone dressed up as the local schoolmaster or policeman!), dancing troupes from neighbouring villages, marching brass bands and on occasion famous colliery bands from Yorkshire and Lancashire; jazz bands, St Bartholomew's Church Band, Scouts, Guides, Boys Brigade, Territorial Army, Cheshire Regiment Band and Platoon, display teams on motorbikes, the British Legion and many other associations who would have been in the procession, a fair with coconut shies, roundabouts for the children, and I think there was a 'boxing booth', but we children were not encouraged to go in! One stall had two 'Brothers Glum', from Poynton or Stockport or somewhere. If you paid your entry fee 1d or $\frac{1}{2}$d for youngsters, and could make them laugh, you received a prize. Not many prizes were ever won – they were very, very good! Competitions were held for the dancing troupes with their paper shaking staffs and ankle decorations,

which all made a wonderful rustling noise.

Wilmslow Carnival attracted many, many visitors as well as residents, and was very, very popular. It was a wonderful day out and resulted in a meaningful amount of money for the hospitals. Everything was given freely and in a wonderful spirit. I could go on and on, but this should give you an idea of what the old days were like!

*Alan Pownall*

## Shopping in the '60s

It was in the '60s that I became a member of staff at Finnigans, a small exclusive department store, not unlike Hoopers, and occupying the same site. This shop was privately owned and boasted a personal rapport between staff and management which in turn was passed on to the customers. The staff were like a huge family, and together with the army of familiar shoppers, filled the building with a unique atmosphere of warmth and relaxation.

Wilmslow was a different town then. There was less traffic, Grove Street wasn't pedestrianised, and it was here that many of the small privately owned shops were to be found. Johnstone's the book shop was a place where you could spend hours browsing, and even longer chatting to the owners who seemed to know every customer as well as every book. There was Sharps the carpet shop, and Woolworths, plus a Mercury Market selling a wide variety of groceries. Moving along, you found Simmons the ironmongers, Henshall's the family butcher, whose choice of meat would have tempted even the most committed vegetarian. Owens the wine shop was an Aladdin's cave of wines and

*An iced-over Black Lake, Lindow Common, Wilmslow.*

spirits, whose ceiling was festooned with grapes and bottles from all over the world, enticing the absolute novice to taste their delights. I remember Edith Dennet as a unique lady – when customers entered her elegant dress shop they were invited to sit down with a cup of coffee, explain what they were looking for, and then as if by magic, a selection of tasteful gowns were produced from the wardrobes that lined the walls. The staff at this shop, like the owner, were knowledgeable and proficient, and many ladies from near and far regularly visited this Grove Street gem. In a similar vein there was Samuel Cooper, who would stand outside his shop on Alderley Road ready to talk to passers by, thus attracting many to step inside. Other beautiful shops were Cloughs (carrying a huge stock of exclusive children's wear) and Severns whose choice of fabrics for the dressmakers of the community was stunning. Mac Fisheries could also be found in Wilmslow at that time, as could Cleggs, Chadwicks, Charnleys and many more. I remember also the coffee bars full of chattering people, and the numerous bread shops whose freshly baked bread filled the air with its luscious aroma.

All these shops had individual character coupled with the personal touch. Today the retail business is much faster, the merchandise has a regimental appearance and for many shops, self-service is the method. The pace of life seems to have quickened, and if, like myself, you can get

*Grove Street.*

away with buying everything in one shop, so much the better. Shopping is a chore for many and only a pleasure for a few. Wilmslow, like so many other towns, is now mainly occupied by retail groups, only a few privately-owned shops remain.

Wilmslow now, I feel, has an industrious feel, as opposed to the suave atmosphere of yesterday.

*Mrs D.L. Warburton*

# Acknowledgements

I would like to extend thanks to:

Miss M. Oughton, for her time, knowledge and advice; Olive Ambrose for pulling out all the stops; Mrs Joan Butcher for tea, biscuits, chat and pictures; Sarah McLelland for her support and enthusiasm; Geoff Bird, for getting me on air; Martin Bell for lunch and a foreword; a 'Wilmslow resident' for her hospitality and an interview; The *Wilmslow Express* and Betty Anderson, for publicity and photography; Alderley Edge Library for the First World War pictures; my husband Tim for his tolerance of late-night printer activity; and to all those who took the time to contribute words and pictures and support.